I0062191

Credit Repair

The Ultimate Guide to Boosting Your Credit Score, Paying off Debt, Saving Money and Managing Your Personal Finances in a Stress-Free Way

Copyright 2019 by Scott Wright - All rights reserved.

The following eBook is reproduced below with the goal of providing information that is as accurate and reliable as possible. Regardless, purchasing this eBook can be seen as consent to the fact that both the publisher and the author of this book are in no way experts on the topics discussed within and that any recommendations or suggestions that are made herein are for entertainment purposes only. Professionals should be consulted as needed prior to undertaking any of the action endorsed herein.

This declaration is deemed fair and valid by both the American Bar Association and the Committee of Publishers Association and is legally binding throughout the United States.

Furthermore, the transmission, duplication, or reproduction of any of the following work including specific information will be considered an illegal act irrespective of if it is done electronically or in print. This extends to creating a secondary or tertiary copy of the work or a recorded copy and is only allowed with express written consent from the Publisher. All additional right reserved.

The information in the following pages is broadly considered to be a truthful and accurate account of facts and as such any inattention, use, or misuse of the information in question by the reader will render any resulting actions solely under their purview. There are no scenarios in which the publisher or the original author of this work can be in any fashion deemed liable for any hardship or damages that may befall them after undertaking information described herein.

Additionally, the information in the following pages is intended only for informational purposes and should thus be thought of as universal. As befitting its nature, it is presented without assurance regarding its prolonged validity or interim quality. Trademarks that are mentioned are done without written consent and can in no way be considered an endorsement from the trademark holder.

Contents

Introduction

When you have a higher credit score, you have many advantages. For example, you can get credit cards with the best rewards, and the lowest rates on any loans.

If you want a mortgage, but you don't have the best credit score, you will have to pay a lot of interest.

A credit score is powerful because it can increase your probability of finding a job or even being accepted as a new tenant because landlords and employers look at your credit score. In other words, a credit score is the best financial estimate to reveal how responsible you are, and it goes to other areas of finance.

Once you are aware of what is on your credit report and how it impacts your score, you have no other choice but to look for ways to repair your credit. Fixing bad credit isn't something that can happen overnight, but again, you don't have to wait years before you see some positive changes.

You don't have to carry the burden of bad credit for your entire life. Begin making a change today by reading this book to learn how to repair your credit card, pay all your debts, save money, and manage all your finances.

Inside this book, you will learn the factors that affect your credit score and how you can fix them. We will also teach you why you need to pay all your debt and some of the ways you can apply to pay your debts. If you have been struggling to learn how to save money, or even how you can manage your finances, read on to discover methods that will allow you to start saving for your future.

Chapter 1: Boosting Your Credit Score

Your credit score has three numbers that lenders use to decide how likely they can be repaid on time if they provide you with a credit card or loan. This is a critical factor when it comes to your financial life. In other words, the higher your credit score is, the more likely you are to qualify for credit cards and loans at the most favorable terms, which saves you some money.

If you have a bad credit history, or it's in a state which you don't want it to be, you aren't alone. Improving your credit score takes time, but the earlier you begin to fix the issues that may be slowing it down, the faster your credit score will rise. It is possible to increase your credit score by taking a few steps, such as building a track record of paying your bills on time, paying down debt, and taking advantage of new tools that will let you add cell phone and utility bills to your credit file.

How to monitor and advance your credit score

When was the last time you looked at your credit? If it is longer than several months, you want to consider checking it. If it's longer than a year, then it's time to change the way you track your credit.

Keeping a close check on your credit enables you to understand the way your financial actions impact your credit. This will also help you to respond to any immediate change in your score and know when you have attained excellent credit, and you may qualify for better interest credit card offers. Alternatively, learning how your credit score changes over time gives you the ability to manage your financial wellbeing. However, it is vital to ensure that you monitor your credit score without damaging it.

Hard and soft inquiries and how they impact your credit

Credit requests, or inquiries about your credit report information, are categorized under soft and hard inquiries. A soft inquiry refers to any inquiry where a prospective lender isn't reviewing your credit. This can take place when you examine your credit score. Don't be scared; soft inquiries don't change your credit score, so don't be afraid to check it.

On the other hand, a hard credit request is when your credit is getting reviewed because you have applied for credit using a prospective lender. Hard inquiries consist of a sizable amount of your general credit score and tend to have the least, short-term effect. However, if you have many of them in the short term, it may indicate that you are a risky borrower. This may lead to a lower credit score.

Get to know your different credit scores

There are two major credit scoring models that lenders can apply to understand the risk:

- The FICO score

- VantageScore

Although each model has the same credit report, they analyze the information differently. Some consumers may check on a considerable difference between the two sources. The score that will be applied depends on the individual lender. However, the FICO Score is widely used. But the VantageScore is often used for free credit scores that you can get online.

Three main credit reporting bureaus or companies search for consumer data and develop credit reports. These credit reports are then used by companies to convert your credit history into a score. The three major bureaus include:

- Experian

- TransUnion

- Equifax

The credit report from each bureau will vary slightly because certain lenders can only report to one while others may report to all three bureaus. In other words, you will have three different FICO Scores, and the score applied will depend on which credit bureau the lender extracts your report from. Despite this, there shouldn't be huge differences among these scores.

Credit Score Monitoring services

There are different credit score monitoring services that you can access easily. You are eligible to a free credit report every year from main credit bureaus. This was an amendment that was done in 2003 in the Fair Credit Reporting Act. The free annual reports can be requested from AnnualCreditReport.com. Despite this, it is critical that you monitor your credit score more than once per year.

Continuous tracking of your credit score will give you the chance to realize any errors done and dispute them early. It will also provide you with a better understanding of the way your financial behavior impacts your credit score in real-time—this gives you the time to work on boosting your credit score. While your score increases, you will notice when it is high to qualify for a lower interest rate and better lending offers.

MyFICO.com provides a paid service that will allow you to track your credit score from different credit bureaus on a quarterly or monthly term. You can get reports from a single or all three bureaus and enjoy extra features, such as theft monitoring and 24/7 fraud resolution, based on the type of monthly subscription you select.

Experian will also provide a credit paid monitoring service for a monthly fee. They will send emails to your inbox every time there is a change in your credit score, along with an explanation so that you can understand your score better.

Credit cards that assist you in tracking your credit score

Your credit card may provide you with a free credit score tracking service. This feature is popular for credit cards designed to fix credit or bad credit cards. But several major credit card providers currently offer this service to all their customers.

Every credit monitoring program has its advantages. The list of issuers that have credit monitoring on most of their credit cards includes Chase, American Express, and Capital One.

If you want to avoid monthly fees, but still stay on top of tracking your credit, you can decide to use the free credit monitoring services from your credit card plus a detailed annual report from AnnualCreditReport.com. You can try the credit monitoring services from MyFICO.com and Experian as well, taking advantage of their free trial. Whichever option you decide to take, it is important that you stay in the loop when handling your credit score and the factors that affect it, and realize that doing so will not affect your credit score.

The three primary credit bureaus and how they operate

The popular credit bureaus have a significant effect on every consumer, but many people don't know these companies or how they work. The top three credit bureaus companies include:

- Experian
- Equifax
- TransUnion

These companies have a great history in the financial industry.

What is a credit bureau?

Also known as a credit reporting agency, it gathers financial information about consumers and combines this information into a single report. Since these bureaus work independently, the credit report that a single bureau generates for an individual could be slightly different from another bureau's report. Although there are smaller credit bureaus, the top three serve a more significant share of the market.

The credit bureaus have a fascinating profit model. Lenders, banks, and many other companies share a lot of information about their clients with credit bureaus for free. The credit bureaus process this information and put it on sale, in the form of a credit report, to different parties that require insight into your financial history, and more.

These credit reports are essential to financial institutions because they assist lenders in knowing individuals who would be profitable clients. If you don't have a credit report, your bank may not know the amount of money that is safe to lend or the interest rate to charge on a loan. For landlords, the credit report acts as an indicator to show whether you can manage to pay rent, and for employers, a good credit report is a symbol of reliability.

Credit reports

Your credit report has some but not all financial data from past and present. A credit report consists of a list of your current and past credit products, the amount of debt you are having, and any late payments or any payment issues that you may have experienced in the recent years. Serious problems such as bankruptcies and tax liens will also show up on the report. However, your credit report will not contain your job history, status of employment, income, and some personal information like your marital status.

Credit scores

Your credit score is determined from a complicated calculation by the credit bureau that summarizes everything from your credit report to show the amount of risk you can bring to lenders. A higher score indicates that you have an excellent payment record. This means that your debt load is low, and you act responsibly to lenders, which means you are a low-risk client. On the other hand, a low credit score implies that you tend to pay your debts late. If you don't have any credit history or it is quite low, then you will have a low score because the credit bureaus will have little information to decide whether you are a risk or not.

Not a single score but many

The challenge with credit scores is that there are different methods to compute them. Therefore, many people have different credit scores based on the type of credit bureau that provides the score. The two major credit scoring models include VantageScore and FICO, but any of these two scoring models come in different forms. Plus, certain items from your financial history may not be taken into account for all three credit bureaus, which can generate a big difference in the scores from those entities.

Making the best from credit bureaus

It is a little annoying to learn that all three credit bureaus have sensitive financial data. However, there's no method to prevent lenders and collection entities from sharing your information with the above companies.

You can limit any possible problems associated with the credit bureaus by evaluating your credit reports annually, and acting immediately in case you notice some errors. It is also good to monitor your credit cards and other open credit products to ensure that no one is misusing the accounts. If you have a card that you don't often use, sign up for alerts on that card so that you get notified if any transactions happen, and regularly review statements for your active cards. Next, if you notice any signs of fraud or theft, you can choose to place a credit freeze with the three credit bureaus and be diligent in tracking the activity of your credit card in the future.

Understanding and boosting your credit score

Whether you have a bad credit score, or you are working to have a credit score, this section is right for you because we shall guide you on how you can build your credit score to help you reach where you want, whether that is boosting your credit score from scratch, or repairing one that is broken.

Your credit health determines your financial future. In other words, when you have strong credit health, you get access to loans with a low-interest rate, and this will save you a lot of bucks in the long term. On the other hand, a bad credit score may limit your chances of getting funds to buy a vehicle, or get the best rates for a credit card.

The credit sector can be complicated, and even challenging to start. The first step to get a strong credit score begins with learning everything about your credit score. By mastering your credit score and the things to do to change it, you will crack your credit potential and realize your goals.

This section will teach you more insights about your credit score, and what you can do to improve it.

The definition of credit score

A credit score has three numbers that reveal much about your credit report, and lenders depend on this to define the health of your credit. An algorithm determines the scores of a credit. This algorithm relies on information from your credit report. Credit scores were developed to show the probabilities that you can achieve in your payment agreement.

There is a misconception that each is allocated a single credit score, which is accessed by lenders and bureaus. This is a lie because you can have multiple credit scores. And the reason is that there are many credit agencies, and different strategies to use to calculate information, and credit scores at different times. If you aren't aware, there are more than a hundred models of scoring, but the most popular models comprise of VantageScore and FICOScore.

Don't be scared about monitoring every credit score, but keep a close eye on the popular scores, which many lenders use to determine whether you qualify for a credit or not.

Learn more about your credit report

A credit report, as the name suggests, contains data and information that credit agencies get from lenders. In the United States, numerous credit agencies process a consumer's credit report. But the main credit agencies that most businesses and financial organizations use include TransUnion, Equifax, and Experian.

Credit reports are updated now and then depending on your credit activity and information you share with financial institutions and businesses. This consists of banks, mortgage firms, credit card firms, and lenders. Information on your credit report can be classified into three categories:

- Credit History

- Public records and collections

- Credit inquiries

Your credit report also has general information that describes more about you. For example, your social security number, name, date of birth and address. Some of the things that your credit report doesn't have include:

- Your occupation, salary, and date of employment (even if lenders want to know this information to approve your loan).

- Your daily spending habits.

Keep in mind that though lenders depend on information in your credit report to learn more about your credit history, there are other aspects not in your credit report that they use to make a decision.

According to the Fair Credit Reporting Act, you have the permission to ask for your credit report at the end of the year from each of the major credit reporting firms.

How is your credit score computed?

Credit bureaus have millions of data to process credit scores, but how do they access this data?

When it comes to matters to do with credit, financial firms such as credit card firms and banks have a dual duty. Many people focus on the role of approving credit. However, that is not the only responsibility they do; they also send out the information to credit bureaus concerning consumer's credit behavior, which is later added into credit reports.

Creditors and lenders who take part in any trade have to share the info about your credit history to the bureaus. This consists of information such as the amount paid, account balance, and the status of your account. A financial company requests each time you sign up for credit and a credit report from a credit bureau—it will be attached to your credit report in the form of a "hard inquiry".

Scoring institutions, such as VantageScore and FICO, require your credit information to determine your credit score. Both VantageScores and FICO extend between 300-850 and include five aspects into the scoring formula. Some of these factors include the age of accounts, credit utilization, types of credit in use, payment history, and new credit.

Top factors that affect your credit score

1. Your payment history

The history of your payment is perhaps one of the most crucial factors that affect your credit score because it will indicate to lenders whether you have been disciplined in making payments on time. This is a great sign to show your probabilities of paying your future debts. As a result, even one or two payments may profoundly affect your credit score.

Dozens of skipped payments can change everything into a "derogatory mark" or "negative record" on your report. If you are only late between 30-60 days, this should not damage your score. However, if you are late for over 90 days, the credit scoring model will interpret that you are likely to repeat it. This is not a great thing because it may easily damage your credit score.

Paying bills on time is one of the best ways that you can apply to adapt and increase your credit score. Think about implementing an automatic bill payment, or installing an online alert on your accounts to monitor your bills and eliminate the risk of skipping a payment.

2. Credit card usage

Your credit usage is also called "debt-to-limit ratio". This ratio determines the size of your whole credit card limit. An ethical principle to follow is to ensure that your credit use ratio doesn't go past 30%. This means the lower the credit card usage, the better. When you have a higher credit card usage ratio, it will reduce your credit score and may cause prospective lenders to become scared that you may not manage more debt.

There are different methods used to reduce the credit use ratio—right from paying a debt to raising the limit on the credit.

3. The age of the credit, and defined credit history

A long history of credit usually changes the score as long as you have a history of making timely payments on the accounts you open.

The factors that are considered include the time the credit accounts were opened, the time specific accounts were opened, and the time elapsed since you used each account.

If you ensure that your oldest credit card remains open, it may increase your score. However, if you have a high fee to pay, it may not improve your score.

It is always a great idea to ensure that your first card is open. Closing the first credit card may affect your credit history and limit your existing credit, which may reduce your credit score.

4. Credit mix and the number of accounts active

The number of active credit accounts plays a big part in your credit score. In summary, a higher number of open credit accounts results in a better credit score. The reason is that a high percentage of your accounts implies that you are approved for credit by more lenders. Additionally, the number of open accounts, the different variety of credit across the main classifications, and the recurring installment loans and revolving credit may increase your credit score.

5. New credit and hard credit inquiries

Every time a person extracts a credit report, the insurer, lender, or landlord is listed on the credit report. There are two categories of credit inquiry:

> • **Hard Inquiries:** This usually happens when a financial mortgage lender, bank, and credit company accesses a report when you register for credit. Hard inquiries are generated with permission to any individual who can generate a credit report, and this is shown on the credit score.

> • **Soft inquiries:** This happens when you access a credit report but not because you are seeking new credit. When you look for a credit report copy, a soft inquiry is generated. Landlords and employers can also send a soft inquiry to deliver a customized quote.

A single hard inquiry is possibly likely to change the score by some points. However, hard inquiries can stay on the credit report for about two years, and this can destroy your score.

Why? The reason is that lenders who notice that you have many recent inquiries may be scared that you are looking at different places because you can't be eligible for the credit. Research indicates that consumers who open numerous credit accounts in a short period pose a big risk of delinquency—especially those without a long-established credit history.

What is considered a good credit score? What is a bad credit score?

So far, you must know that a credit score is a good metric of financial health. It demonstrates your level of trust to financial companies and can assist in determining how expensive and easy it can be for you to purchase a home, car, or even rent an apartment. Good credit may assist you in securing a date.

That is why it is important, if possible, to consider actions to improve your score. However, the factors that define a good or bad credit aren't broadly understood. About 25% of millennials don't understand what a good credit score is; this is based on the survey done by LendEdu.

Typically, businesses and lenders define their parameters for measuring a model they want to use and what makes up for a good score for a specific service or product. A specific score isn't an assurance for credit approval or even gets the lowest rates, but you need to focus on a better score that will increase the probability that you will get the best rates.

According to the Credit bureaus Experian, it has various score ranges, as shown below:

Credit Score	Rating	% of People	Impact
300-579	Very Poor	17%	Credit applicants may be required to pay a fee or deposit, and applicants with this rating may not be approved for credit at all.
580-669	Fair	20.20%	Applicants with scores in this range are considered to be subprime borrowers, meaning their credit standing is less than what is normally desired.
670-739	Good	21.50%	Only 8% of applicants in this score range are likely to become seriously delinquent in the future.
740-799	Very Good	18.20%	Applicants with scores here are likely to receive better than average rates from lenders.
800-850	Exceptional	19.90%	Applicants with scores in this range are at the top of the list for the best rates from lenders.

Keep in mind that the consumer percentage in each of the five credit score ranges is on average equal, and at around 20%. What makes up for "good" credit starts with a credit score of about 670. At this score level, you will qualify for approval on different loan types; this means you can have a higher rate of payment than a person with "very good" or "exceptional" credit.

Taking the right steps to boost your score can assist you in being eligible for a credit that has better rates, and also eliminate extra deposits that borrowers require when they have lower scores.

In case you see that your score isn't okay, take the time to check your credit report to see if there are any methods you can use to change your credit score over time. If you realize that your credit score is low because of inaccurate information, you can consider disputing the error.

Why your credit score is vital?

In the course of your life, there will be different times where people and businesses will depend on your score to help them decide whether you are a good fit to do business with and the types of rates you deserve. When you have a great credit score, it will provide you with many opportunities and savings. Below are some of the things that a good credit score may help you achieve:

- **Big ticket loans through traditional financial companies**

If you have been searching for a larger-sized financing option for your small business loan, your first stop may be a bank. Many people waste hours completing paperwork and gathering information for the loan application, but one of the main features of the information that plays a key part in whether you are approved for a loan or not is your credit score. This means that if you plan to get in the market for a large loan, then you will want to ensure that your credit score is in great shape. A great score will help you to qualify, and this can assist you in securing the best rates, which may lead to thousands in savings.

- **Credit cards**

Even when you have a poor credit score, it will still be easy to receive a credit card, but the options will be limited. When you have a higher credit score, you will easily qualify for various credit cards that provide customers with sign-up bonuses, entry to airport lounges, and many more. Start developing a strong credit history of timely payments so that you don't miss some of these best rewards.

- **Car financing**

For many Americans, purchasing a car is one of the best goals they can make in their life. And this can be realized when you have a good credit score. In other words, people with a good credit score have a better chance of being awarded the best rates for a car loan. Aiming to have a better credit score before you walk into the car dealership may help you save thousands of dollars in interest.

- **Online loans**

Online lenders have turned out to be the best option for traditional financial firms and are known for using technology and data to offer quick loans and make a decision on rates. Plus, they simplify the online activity. Online lenders such as Upgrade implement soft credit evaluations in case you are pre-approved for a personal loan. A strong credit score may provide you with alternative options and attractive rates of interest with online lenders.

• Insurance

A strong credit score and healthy credit record can assist you in earning an affordable insurance premium compared to others who have an average or poor credit record. Why? The reason is that insurance wants information that may help them to determine the risk of an applicant, and the probability that they will go delinquent on the payment of the insurance. Your credit score is a means to check risk and build a policy and premium at a cost that is in line with the level of risk they define. A great credit score may help you secure the best insurance policy at a better rate. And this will provide you and your loved ones some peace of mind.

• Cell phone service

One of the first things that cell phone service providers do when they want to decide whether to deliver cellular service is to confirm the history of the credit. If your credit score fails to fulfill their requirements, they might request you to make a down payment, provide you with a smaller phone selection to select from, and offer the best promotional rates. It is difficult for many people to think of life without a cell phone, but don't allow your credit score to hinder you.

• The keys to an apartment

Many landlords have to evaluate your credit before they can finalize the process of apartment application. For that reason, a good credit score will be advantageous from other apartment seekers in the competitive market.

How you can build your credit from scratch

Maybe you have just begun life, or maybe you have put a stop to using credit. What is the best method to build a good credit score if you don't have any at the moment?

Well, here are some strategies to try:

Look for a loan with a cosigner

> • **Period**: At least six months of timely payments.

> • **Level of difficulty:** It depends on your potential to get a great cosigner.

> • **Who is it best for?** A person with a cosigner with high credit and ready to cosign.

This requires that you register for a loan, but look for another person to cosign the loan to convince the lender to approve it. If you don't have any credit, the loan will be created based on the history and financial potential of the cosigner.

This can go well if you are approved as a cosigner. The person may have to be ready to cosign your loan and possess the potential to qualify. If you don't have a person who can fulfill these requirements, it will not be an option.

Once you get the loan and make early payments, the lender will have to report your payment history to the credit bureaus. This will allow you to build a credit score slowly.

The drawback is that paying late affects your credit and the cosigner's credit score. In case you default, the cosigner will be asked to pay off the loan.

The best kind of loan to use this method is an auto loan. The cosigner agreements are popular with auto loans, but with an installment loan, it will generate a massive weight compared to credit cards.

Choose a "credit builder loan" – two or three

Period: Six months to one year.

Level of difficulty: Easy.

Who is it best for? A person that has at least a few hundred dollars available.

This has turned out to be a common trend in recent times, and it's present with many credit unions and banks. If you don't have a credit score, you can choose a credit builder loan, which is similar to a secured loan.

For instance, let's assume you have $500 and you want to deposit that into a savings account using a credit union. The credit union can generate a credit card using the line protected by a savings account, for around $500.

While you use the credit line and pay your monthly payments, the credit union will report the payments to the credit bureaus. Later on, they will build a credit score. This can be helpful in acquiring a second or even third credit builder loan. This will offer you multiple credit references.

With the presence of these loans, a lender can release your savings account in case you have great payment history, and the protected credit line may become unsecured. This will make it become a traditional credit card.

Become authorized to use someone else's credit card

Period: Six to twelve months.

Level of difficulty: Average because of different variables.

Who is it best for? People with less or no credit.

This method is like a mixed bag. The basic premise is that the main cardholder includes you as an authorized person to use the card. In other words, you can make charges on the card, but you aren't accountable for the payments.

This helps build a credit score, but it's subject to different aspects, and some aren't known when the arrangement is made:

- Some credit card issuers don't disclose account activity on authorized users.

- Credit scoring models may generate less weight to authorized user status, and hence, it may not feature the beneficial effect you could hope for.

- The arrangements may be helpful in case the account is in a good state. In case there are late payments by the main user, or the account balance is high, it may affect your effort, and your credit score.

- Because you aren't a primary cardholder, you may have little control over how you manage the account. This can succeed if the account is controlled, but hurt if it isn't.

Find a student credit card

Period: Six to twelve months.

Level of difficulty: Fairly simple.

Who is it best for? Students and young adults with little or no credit.

The student credit cards will allow you to start building a credit score early in life. Most provide associated services, such as information on how to control and enhance your credit.

One of the most common student credit cards is the Discover it Cash Back Card. This card provides 1% cash back on all purchases, 5% cash back on revolving purchase types, and a $20 annual bonus for better grades. The card has no annual fee and even offers you a free monthly FICO score.

To qualify for a student credit card can be challenging. If you are below 21 years of age and want to own a credit card, you will need to know how to create evidence of income to ensure you qualify for approval. You may always get approved with a part-time job. You also need to have little or no credit history without derogatory information. These cards aren't meant for people with impaired credit.

But if you can't manage to get an independent income, you will have to qualify as an authorized user on the card, with your parents as the main cardholders.

When you successfully get a student credit card, make sure that you use it responsibly. This will only assist you in growing your credit if you maintain a low balance and make timely payments. If you become sloppy and use it without any measures in place, you will perhaps have a bad credit history. And this is something that you don't want to experience in life.

Letting rent and utilities report your payment history

Period: Six to twelve months.

Level of difficulty: Depends on the strategy you use.

Who is it best for? Individuals without credit, or those that have bad credit but want to include good credit references.

Traditionally, both rent and utility payments used to work against you when it comes to credit. Neither landlords nor utility companies could reveal you have a good credit history to the credit bureaus. However, if you are aware that you have a past due balance, that will be reported to the bureaus.

Rent reporting: There are various services that one can apply to in order to get rent payments included on their credit report. Plus, unique methods on how this happens. One service includes Experian RentBureau—this will indicate your rent as a trade line, and factor in payments for the last 25 months.

The challenge is to find a landlord with whom you can report your rent history to the service. There are some charges that you need to pay, which may make the landlord reluctant. Additionally, if your landlord doesn't want to work together, you will have to begin making your rent payments to a rental collection service, which will include a certain charge. There are a wide variety of rent collection agencies, each with its own fee structure.

Another option is Rental Kharma. While this is not a rent collection service, it will still report your payment history to TransUnion. These confirm your lease and check to make sure that every payment has been made on time. You can also register for a canceled rent check for the last 24 months to assist the process along.

This kind of service will only be active if you make timely rent payments every time and every month. Luckily, many landlords will not report a late payment unless it persists for more than 30 days.

Find utility companies to report to the credit bureaus

In 2015, FICO released a new scoring model that featured utility payments. This one comprised of utility companies, as well as internet and cell phone services.

This is considered an alternative scoring model, and it applies to people who don't have a credit score. If you already have bad credit, this scoring model may not be helpful.

The other problem is the general absence of acceptance by creditors. Just a few lenders apply the FICO model. Mortgage lenders and possibly auto lenders could frequently apply it; however, its application among credit card issuers is scarce.

Alternatively, the presence of this alternative option is not included in the traditional scores of FICO.

It is possibly worth it to try it, but whether or not it's going to work will depend on your payment history using utility companies, and more importantly, whether a given lender makes use of this particular FICO score. And perhaps, if you are a student or a young person living with your parents, you will not have rent and utilities to report.

For that reason, utilities and rent have a minimum value as credit references in most situations, especially for students.

Register for credit cards for people without credit

Period: Six to twelve months.

Level of difficulty: Fairly easy.

Who is it best for? People with at least $200.

As with credit builder loans, these are protected cards. Most of these cards are offered by lenders whom you have never heard of. They operate the same style as the credit builder loans, but the credit lines are a bit smaller. Most of them have a starting credit line of $200, which may need an equal security deposit.

You'll use the cards. and pay the monthly payments, and your payment history will be sent to the credit bureaus. This will allow you to improve your credit scores slowly.

The drawback of these cards is that they have a higher fee. For instance, a lender may offer a credit limit of $200, but charge interest of $50. This will decrease your credit limit to around $150, which won't provide you much in terms of spending potential.

These cards are recommended to people who can't find a cosigner for a loan or don't have money for a credit builder loan.

The best way to boost your credit score isn't currently where you want it to be

Let's assume you already got a credit score, but it is below what you want it to be. What are some of the best means to make your credit score better?

Pay off any past debts

Period: Within 30 days.

Level of difficulty: Easier if you already have the funds; impossible if you don't.

Who is it best for? Anyone with past debts or balances.

These may comprise of due balance on active accounts, charge-offs, old debts, and tax liens.

If you have any outstanding charges, clearing them is one of the best ways you can change your credit score. Begin by first paying the smallest ones. For the big balances, enter into a negotiation with the creditor to accept less than the complete amount.

Any pay offs should comprise of a paper trail. This can be a canceled check or even a letter of satisfaction from the creditor.

However, paying off a past due balance doesn't eliminate you from the negative list from your credit report. However, a paid collection is often better than an unpaid one, so you will still be going in the right direction.

Dispute your credit errors

Period: It depends on your credit history.

Level of difficulty: It changes between moderate to more difficult.

Who is it best for? Any person with errors on their credit report.

Find a copy of your credit report, one from the top three credit bureaus. Remember that you are eligible for a free report at the end of twelve months.

Analyze the three credit reports. If you see any errors, you will have to get in touch with the reporting creditor and get the information fixed. You will possibly be required to provide documents to show the derogatory entry is a mistake. If you manage to prove your case, you will get a letter from the creditor to confirm the correction and make sure that they report it to all the three credit bureaus.

This is not an easy thing to do, but it is one of the quickest methods you can use to improve your credit scores. Any form of derogatory content you delete will increase your credit score.

However, it's important that you avoid going for a credit repair service because the reputation of members in that sector is questionable and expensive.

Make timely payments of all your obligations from now on

Period: At least twelve months, or even more.

Level of difficulty: This one will depend on your financial condition and level of commitment.

Who is it best for? Everyone.

Not only is this obvious, but you may not proceed if you aren't done with this one yet. In other words, from now onwards, pay all your monthly bills on time. And not only monthly bills, but also your debts. When talking about monthly payments, we refer to subscriptions, utilities, rent, phone services, and many more. You must develop a habit of good credit.

Track your credit from now on

Period: Ongoing.

Level of difficulty: It is easy until you find a new error.

Who is it best for? Everyone, no matter the credit level.

Once you have errors fixed, it is important to continue tracking your credit. Just like the way errors continue to show up in the past, they may continue to occur in the future. That means you will have to remain on top of this state. And that requires that you track your credit now and then.

If you are wondering how you can achieve this, a few credit score providers will assist you. One of them is Credit Karma. If you didn't know, Credit Karma is one of the most common and well known among free credit score generators. Credit Karma will provide your VantageScore3.0 from Equifax and TransUnion. They also deliver details about your credit score factors that resemble a complete credit report.

If you discover a massive drop in your score, it is probably because of some derogatory information that has been included in your credit report. You can start a dispute if the information is an error. This is often done when the error first shows up so that you have a fresh memory and required documentation is easily available.

Pay your high credit card balances

Period: Within 30 days.

Level of difficulty: Simple if you have the cash to do it, but hard when you don't.

Who is it best for? Anyone who has a high credit card balance.

Do you recall credit utilization? One of the easiest means to boost your credit scores is by cutting down your ratio and paying all your due balances. If you can bring down the ratio to 50% from 80%, the better your credit scores will be.

Apply some wonderful credit to the mix

Period: It depends on your credit history, but a minimum of twelve months.

Level of difficulty: It depends on your credit history.

Who is it best for? Everyone.

If you have a huge percentage of negative information on your credit report, you may have to counter that by applying a lot of good credit. Follow the same method as you would if you are focused on building credit scores from the start:

- Pay bills on time from this day going forward.

- Look for a credit builder loan.

- Get a consigned loan.

For bad credit, time can be your friend as long as you pay all your bills on time. A piece of derogatory credit information will disappear from your report after seven years. However, if you decide to shave off your old bad credit, and establish a pattern of good new credit, your credit scores will start to increase in less than seven years.

Easy steps to use to repair your credit and improve your credit score

Rebuilding your credit isn't that difficult, and boosting your credit score may not necessarily take months.

Fixing your credit score may generally imply qualifying for a lower interest charge and better terms. This is true regardless of whether you want a good credit score to request money for personal reasons, or you can buy inventory, and lease a facility to begin growing your business.

The issue is that credit repair is a bit like growing your professional network—you only start to think about it when it is important. However, when you don't have good credit, it becomes hard to fix the same situation overnight.

That is the reason the time to begin fixing your credit is now—before the time comes where you really need it. Luckily, it is not that hard to improve your credit score. Below are some easy processes that you can implement:

1. Dispute any late payments

Errors do happen. Your mortgage lender may send a report that a certain payment was late when in reality you paid it on time. A credit card provider may enter the wrong payment.

You are allowed to dispute these payments, whether in accounts that are current or have already been closed. It is not different from the way you challenge your derogatory marks.

Your payment profile is a great factor in your credit score, so you should remain committed to clean up the mistakes.

2. Choose whether you also want to play the games certain credit repair companies play

So far, you have learned about removing inaccurate information, but did you know that you can also decide to dispute accurate information?

For instance, let's assume that an account went to collection, you failed to pay it, and the collection entity fails to come for collection. All that is left is the record on your credit report. You can still decide to dispute this entry—many do. And there are occasions where the entries are removed.

Why? The reason is that once you start a dispute, the credit bureau will request the creditor to confirm the information. Some will, but most collection agencies don't. Instead, they ignore the request, and the agency has to clear the entry from your credit report.

In other words, smaller companies, or midsize providers, are highly likely to respond to credit bureaus. It is a task they don't need. Credit card firms, auto finance firms, banks, and mortgage lenders are highly likely to respond.

So, if you want, but this is not a recommendation, it's a method some individuals employ—you can go ahead and dispute information hoping that the creditor will not respond. This is a method that most credit repair firms use to improve the credit score of their clients. If the creditor fails to respond, the entry is omitted.

Now the question is: Should you go for this approach? That is for you to decide.

3. Make a humble request

Say you attempted to remove the derogatory comment, account marked "Paid as agreed", but failed. Should you now give up? Or give it another try?

Don't give up; you can instead make a humble request or even ask interestingly.

Creditors have the authority to allow credit bureaus to eliminate records from your credit report at any time. So when all else doesn't work, call and make a humble request. You will be surprised to learn how a humble request may assist you.

4. Increase the limits of your credit

Another important factor that plays a key role in your credit score is your credit card usage. This ratio often causes a massive change. In general, a large balance of over 50% on your existing credit will adversely affect your score. Mixing your cards will probably affect your score.

One method that you can use to ensure that you have a good ratio is to clear your balances, but another method is to increase the limit of your credit.

To have the limit/s increased, you need to call and ask politely. If you have a good payment history, most credit card companies are going to be happy to increase your limit.

Even as they increase your limit, remain disciplined so that you don't use extra available credit—if you do so, you will return to the original credit ratio boat. And you will be in big debt.

5. Open a new credit card account

You can also positively increase your credit score by choosing to open a new account. Your only goal is to make sure that there is no balance on this card, and the credit available will possibly rise depending on the limit.

Get a card that doesn't require you to pay an annual fee. Your best route has to be through a bank—of which you already have a bank account with. The cards that don't have a yearly charge tend to demand high-interest rates, but if you don't leave a balance, this may not affect you.

However, again, you need to be smart. Your target shouldn't be to have more cash but to improve the credit score. If you think you may easily use the balance on the new account, then it is better that you don't open another one.

6. Clear high-interest "new" credit accounts first

The era of credit is important to your credit report. The interest rates are important to your bank account. Let's assume you have $100 to pay down balances every month; then you must focus on clearing high-interest accounts first. Next, you can prioritize based on the age of the account. Pay the recent ones first so that you can increase the average period of the credit, which should assist you in scoring, but you will also have the ability to avoid paying off high-interest rates.

Then you can place the money that you haven't spent on that payment into another account on your list.

7. Don't throw away your old credit cards

The length of time that you have used your credit history has a moderate but useful credit score. Let's say you own a credit card for ten years. If you decide to close that account, it may reduce your general credit profile and affect your score negatively, especially in the short term.

If you are planning to raise your credit score but at the same time close your credit account, focus on closing your "newest" card.

Do it yourself credit repair: Steps to repair bad credit on your own

It is crucial that you don't fall for scams that promise easy, overnight credit repair. If you want to correct your bad credit, you can do it yourself. These simple steps will help you boost your credit score.

So far, you know that when you have poor credit, you won't qualify for new credit products, such as credit cards. Though you may manage to get an auto loan or even a mortgage, you are going to pay a high interest rate because of the poor credit score. This is unlike a person with a better credit score. Here are some potential ways to fix your credit:

1. Know where you stand

Before you start the DIY repair, you want to have complete copies of your credit reports from the three bureaus—Equifax, Experian, and TransUnion.

As mentioned, these reports are free as long as you request them once a year from www.annualcrediteport.com. Other websites may promise to grant you a free report, but that is just a lie.

2. If you get errors, dispute them

The next process in your credit repair is to file a dispute for incorrect information captured on your report. Mistakes are common, so if you see any errors, whether small or big, it is important to clear them. And here is what you need to do:

Once you receive a full copy of your credit report, verify your identity information, and your credit history.

Verify the list of credit cards, debts, and main transactions. If you notice any mistake, then you need to create a copy of the report and highlight the mistake.

Next, collect any information that you may need to provide as evidence; it could be your bank statements. This is very critical because credit bureaus will not act on anything if there is no proof.

3. Prevent the bleeding

Once you finish fixing any errors found on your credit report, this is the time to make sure that you don't spend more than what you can generate every month.

Why is this so critical? It's because there are just three simple things to do to fix a bad credit:

- Pay bills on time

- Pay your debt

- Don't apply for credit

Of course, before you can begin to do any of the listed things, you have to make sure that you don't spend more than what you earn. In other words, you must have a budget.

First, analyze the returns of your tax for the last two years to get a clue of how much money you earn at the end of the year.

Deduct your monthly expenses from your present income. Next, you need to create an estimate of how much money you spend every month on other costs, such as entertainment, gas, and groceries. After this, you should build a limit that is based on your income, and what you can spend in each of the various categories of costs.

How to get late payments deleted like the pros

Late payments cause a huge negative impact on your credit scores. If you didn't know, these payments could remain on your credit reports for seven years, so you need to do everything you can to prevent getting them.

If there are any instances of a late payment on your credit report, you will have to do something to remove it and boost your credit scores. And in case you make a late payment, there's that opportunity to have it removed.

But why do late payments appear on credit reports?

There are two reasons for this:

> 1. You aren't at fault. In this case, the late payment is a mistake.

> 2. You are at fault. You probably paid late.

In the first scenario, you can remove the late payment from your credit reports by filing a dispute. Credit bureaus want to have accurate information on their records, so when you file a dispute, they will look into it so they can fix the issue.

In the second instance, you may manage to get the late payment removed from the credit reports. However, this process involves applying polite language and sending a humble request. You may also need to describe your condition and promise to be disciplined and responsible in the coming years. However, this method does not guarantee that you will succeed.

Regardless of the late payment on your credit reports, it is worth it to take the time to remove it. You're going to learn when late payments will appear on your credit reports, and why it is important to remove them. Finally, you will learn how to dispute an inaccurate late payment, and how you can request lenders to wipe out records of late payments.

Point to note

When searching for credit companies to fix your credit score, you will come across multiple companies that will promise to do the service "fast" and for a price. Some may even promise to remove any negative features on your credit report. The truth is: everything these companies do, you can do it yourself; they have no special access.

While you may want to work with some of those companies, ensure that they are reputable. That way, you will save your time and energy to look for all contact details and documents to file a dispute. Instead, you can get a person who has experienced this before, and who can guide you on what to expect and speed up the whole process.

If you know that you aren't at fault, dispute the payment

As mentioned, this method is perfect if there is an incorrect late payment on your credit records that never occurred.

You can also apply this method if you did make a late payment, but there's some false information related to it. However, in this situation, you perhaps shouldn't expect a late payment record to be completely removed. But they will correct the error, and you'll still have the late payment remain there.

It is free to file a dispute of data in your credit report. You may consider disputing the late payment with various companies. Below is a basic structure:

1. Highlight the problem. Make sure you confirm the credit report that the late payment has shown up on.

2. Get in touch with the creditor to find out whether they will correct the error and alert credit bureaus.

3. Get in touch with credit bureaus. If it's important, get in touch with the credit bureaus to dispute late payments.

Learn to be patient. This procedure may successfully end at the second step, or it may even take longer. You don't have to experience many problems with the popular credit card issuers if they actually made an error, even if that demands that you spend a lot of time on the phone. But there is a chance that other credit card companies may be quite hard to work with, especially sub-prime cards companies.

1. Review your credit reports

If you think you may have an incorrect late payment, the first step is to verify all your credit reports to see whether it is captured on all records.

While you review your late payments, you should pay attention to the account number, lender, the amount paid, the data, and so forth.

Though this step is not that important—because credit bureaus will pull out your late payment accounts when you begin an online dispute with them—when you review your credit reports, you will have a better insight into your accounts, and when the late payment happened. And in case there is a big error on your reports, such as a late payment, it is important to check to make sure everything is accurate.

Below are some free methods to use to look at your credit reports. However, assessing your reports may not have a huge problem regarding your credit scores at all. Some of these services will provide you with comprehensive information compared to others.

1. Apply a credit monitoring service

There are different services that you can use. They don't offer you the actual credit reports, but they can display the information the reports have. Some of those services include:

- Credit.com for Equifax and TransUnion reports.

- CreditKarma for the Experian and TransUnion reports.

- Experian free membership. This is meant for little information related to your Experian report.

- Capital One CreditWise for the TransUnion report.

- The Chase Credit Journey meant for TransUnion reports.

i) You can visit AnnualCreditReport.com to receive a free copy of your credit report per year.

ii) You may qualify for extra free credit reports.

2. Dispute the lender

Once you note that there is a false late payment on one or more of your credit reports, then it could be time to get in touch with the lender who sends the report.

If they are a credit card issuer, it will be easy as calling the number written on the back of your card, or reviewing the list of credit company contact details. If not, you may have to look for the right contact information to call the lender.

You may be lucky to succeed in calling and alerting them to the error. They may review their records, and identify the mistake, and take the necessary steps to correct it.

In some cases, the lender could ask for a request to show proof that you didn't make any late payment. They may even ask for a letter that has a copy of a bank statement indicating the payment, or any form of documentation. If they are satisfied, they will fix the error.

When the lender accepts that the late payment is an error, it is important to put it in writing. Find a written verification that shows the late payment reporting error from the lender, and not your mistake.

Next, ask the lender to file a dispute of the late payment with the credit agencies and have it purged out from your credit report. If they can't dispute it, then you may have to do it on your own.

Regardless of whether the lender will send the dispute or you will do it on your own, you have to make sure that you review your reports after every month so that you can verify the late payment is fixed.

Another thing that the lender has to do once it is proven that it's an error is to refund any late payments that you made.

The lender may accept that it was an error, but that doesn't imply that the late payment will instantly vanish from your reports. In particular, when the lender doesn't file for disputes with the credit bureaus, you will have to implement this step by yourself.

If you fail to show that you made payments on time, you may be unfortunate. But still, you can go ahead and start a dispute with the credit bureaus if you are sure the late payment is a mistake.

3. Disputing with the credit bureaus

Disputes can be done online, or even via mail or cell phone. When you file a dispute for an item on your credit report, the credit bureau has to launch an investigation that may take longer. The bureau will have to analyze the information and confirm with the lender if it is necessary. Once they prove that the item is correct, it will have to remain on the credit report. If they find that the item is incorrect, they will remove it from your report.

Keynote

If you make a late payment, don't file a dispute as inaccurate. Some people attempt this, hoping to get some luck when the creditor fails to verify in time. This is making false claims and may destroy your relationship with the credit card issuer, and they may fail to approve you for cards in the future.

It is advised that you dispute online; that way, it will be faster, and more accurate. Every credit bureau has a free online dispute system that you can apply to.

If you dispute through email, make sure that you send the information listed below. This could be really helpful even though it looks too much:

- A copy of your utility bank, bill, or insurance statement.

- Your date of birth.

- Your Social Security Number.

- An address to show where you have lived in the last two years.

- Your full names.

- Any supportive documentation, such as a notice from the lender that the late payment is inaccurate, or even a bank statement to indicate the timely payment.

Make sure you send copies of documents, and not the original versions because you won't get them back. You don't have to write a long, detailed explanation of your condition; however, the more evidence you provide, the better.

You are the one at fault

If you know that you made a late payment, you still have a chance to have it purged from your credit report. This may be a slim opportunity, but it is important to try because a late payment has a major impact on your credit.

These methods require you to contact the creditor, instead of the credit bureaus. You will basically be pleading your case and requesting them to pardon you the late payment. The creditors have no condition to do so. If they choose to report the account as current rather than a delinquent, this is often referred to as "goodwill adjustment".

This may succeed if you do have a great payment history with the lender, and you have been a disciplined customer except for this single mistake. If a technical error hindered you from paying on time—for example, a problem with the payment system—that may work to your favor. Or, say there was a massive life event that hindered you from paying on time, they could be sympathetic to that.

If you haven't been a great customer, and you have a history of late payments plus other negative comments, you may not have much success with the "goodwill adjustment". However, it could be worth trying it based on your condition because it will not cost you anything.

You have only two steps for the following process:

    1. Ask nicely

    2. Negotiate

Goodwill adjustment using a phone call or letter

You can attempt a goodwill adjustment using two methods: mail and phone. Some people only try one, while some attempt both. Typically, many people tend to have success from calling and sending multiple letters over time, but this cannot be confirmed.

Whether you are on the phone or you write a letter, keep in mind that you are at fault here and it is important to ask for forgiveness. The tone you speak with should reflect that too. Be thankful, polite, and conscientious. Besides this, don't get demanding or angry.

Below are some examples to help you start a phone conversation or a goodwill letter. If you do find a positive response from the creditor, you should try to get it in writing.

Phone

Use the script below to begin a conversation about clearing your late payment. Just confirm that you have your explanation for why you were late. If you don't have a great payment history, you may have to adjust it gradually to reveal your initial state.

LATE PAYMENT GOODWILL ADJUSTMENT SAMPLE PHONE SCRIPT

"Hello, my name is [your name]. I recently made a late payment on my account, which was a total accident.

As you can see, my payment history is perfect other than this one mistake. I ended up paying late because [insert your explanation here]. The late payment is also showing up on my credit reports.

Is there any way you could remove this late payment from the record, by reporting that account as always current?"

This should get you started in the right way.

Mail

Take the time to write a great, old-fashioned letter. A goodwill letter has to be customized to reflect the current situation and the good intention to be a disciplined credit user.

Accept your mistake for the late payment, and don't make excuses. Explain some of the conditions surrounding it, whether it was about your potential to pay, some confusion, or some other reason. Highlight that you have been making other payments on time. If there is something that hindered you from a timely payment, explain that it's not a problem now.

The sample letter below should work as a great template to get you started. Make sure you adjust it where possible to fit your condition.

LATE PAYMENT GOODWILL ADJUSTMENT SAMPLE LETTER TO CREDITOR

[Date]

[Your Name]

[Your Address]

[Your Phone Number]

[Your Email Address]

[Your Account Number]

Complaint Department

[Name of Creditor]

[Creditor Address]

Dear Sir or Madam:

I hope you're doing well today. My name is [your name], and I've been a satisfied customer of [creditor] for [number] of years. I've always made my payments on time, but unfortunately I recently made a mistake on [date].

I understand how important it is to make timely payments. However, I missed my payment because [brief explanation of why you missed your payment]. But I'm confident this won't happen again. As you can see from my credit history, I have a long record of on-time payments before and since the late payment.

As a courtesy, I respectfully request that you make a goodwill adjustment to remove the late payment on [date]. Please consider my track record as proof that I take my financial obligations seriously.

If you have any questions, or if you would like to speak with me in more detail, please call me at [your phone number] or send me an email at [your email address here].

Thank you for your consideration,

[Your name]

Try to negotiate

If a regular goodwill adjustment fails to deliver the expected results, you can attempt to negotiate. You could have some leverage to work with, but maybe not.

There are different types of offers that you could make:

- *Autopay:* This is where you set up an automatic payment system so that the creditor can receive timely payment.

- *Payment plan:* You need to agree to pay a given amount each month to pay off a current balance.

- *Partial settlement:* This one requires you to pay the outstanding balance, and agree to pay off the rest over time.

- *Complete settlement:* Pay off the remaining balance with the creditor.

Attempt any negotiating technique that you know; you may be lucky if you can demonstrate that you're financially able to make the payment every month.

To include the negotiation technique in your phone call or goodwill letter, you only need to insert one of these scripts into the conversation. Or you can combine them in a certain way.

AUTOPAY

On my part, I'll sign up for the autopay system so you can be sure that you'll always get my payments on time. I have a good job with a steady income, so I'm not worried about missing future payments.

PAYMENT PLAN

On my part, I'll pay off my remaining balance of [your account balance] over the next [number of months] months, making payments of [payment amount] each month. I'll sign up for autopay so you can be sure that you'll always get my payments on time. I have a good job with a steady income, so I'm not worried about missing future payments.

PARTIAL SETTLEMENT

On my part, I'll pay [payment amount] of my outstanding balance now, and will pay off the rest over the next [number of months] months. I'll sign up for the autopay system so you can be sure that you'll always get my payments on time. I have a good job with a steady income, so I'm not worried about missing future payments.

FULL SETTLEMENT

On my part, I'll pay off my entire balance of [your account balance] now to show my commitment. I intend to remain a loyal customer. I have a good job with a steady income, so I'm not worried about missing future payments.

How to find Credit cards with guaranteed approval?

If you have been struggling to get a credit card because you already have bad credit, you may be asking yourself about the guaranteed approval card offers you have seen. Are they genuine? And what exactly does guaranteed approval really mean? Although this term may seem like the solution to your credit card problems, the truth is that all credit cards have certain basic requirements before a company can release one to you. One key thing with the guaranteed approval is that there are minimum requirements set for one to qualify.

Many issuers of guaranteed approval require a person to have an active checking account and to show evidence of income that it surpasses a specific minimum amount. There is also the issue of how bad your credit is. In general, a credit score of between 300 and 650 is bad credit. But some card issuers will view a score of 550-650 as poor credit, and they may consider you for an unsecured credit card.

The process of signing up for guaranteed approval credit cards is done online. These credit cards will provide you with immediate approval. Also, they are meant for people with bad credit.

For those that have bad credit, it is easy to be deceived by these offers. However, before you move forward and sign up, consider the following tips:

1. Don't submit many applications

Don't send multiple applications for guaranteed approval. This may damage your credit.

2. Have a repayment plan

When you are approved, do you have an effective repayment plan? Don't get into a state of being unprepared. The best thing to recall as a credit card holder is to stay up to date with your bills no matter the type of credit card you have. Will your monthly income let you pay additional expenses? Or it is practical to improve your credit first before you receive a credit card?

3. Plan for other options

When you have different options, it will help you increase the score of your credit card. Some of these options include a department store and gas station card. It is easy to get these cards, and they do the same work as credit cards.

4. Be ready to pay off your balance completely

If you choose to own a bad credit card, you have to be ready to fulfill your obligations of paying for it. Don't let anything discourage you from paying your credit card debts. Make sure that you note down your payment dates.

5. Read before signing

This is very important; you need to read each statement found on the terms and conditions of your credit card. Be sure that you have understood everything. If there are questions, don't be afraid to call the bank and speak to a representative. It is important to be confidently aware that you don't have hidden charges or vague clauses in your credit card.

Chapter 2: Paying Off debt

Lies about Debt

Today's society has spread a bunch of lies about the debt that we have come to believe as true. Some of us have believed them to the point where many of us are already in debt.

But how can we stop believing these lies and start to dwell on the truth? One way is by educating ourselves and learning what debt is and what it is not.

Many different lies have been propagated about debt. Let's take a look at some of them:

1. Find a credit card to build your credit

This perception that you have to look for a credit to grow credit implies that you have to have debt so that after some time you can increase your debt. It is ridiculous. The idea of purchasing a home later on emerges. So, can you get a house without a credit card? The lenders will say no, but this is not true.

You can get a mortgage from a firm that is involved in underwriting. This means that you don't just focus on your credit score but look at your financial history. You may be eligible for mortgages if you have paid your bills on time for the last two years, have a great history of paying your utilities on time, or have been in the same career for a minimum of two years, and have an excellent record of payment.

You may think this is very difficult—only because someone told you about an alternative route. The truth is that you don't need to apply for credit to purchase a home. An excellent history of financial stewardship will help you get a home when the time comes to buy one.

2. All debt is bad

This negative perception associated with debt has caused a large number of people to begin thinking that all debt is bad. While irresponsible borrowing isn't a great thing, a well-handled debt can become positive and assist you in building your credit history and enhancing your credit score.

This will increase the credit score to boost your chances of getting credit in the future and securing big loans such as mortgages.

Also, a mortgage can be said to be good debt because it aids in getting a long-term investment.

3. Debt consolidation repairs our issues with debt

Debt consolidation is a significant issue because it hides a huge problem. From a purely financial standpoint, it may look like a great idea; however, the challenge is that we are the ones who drive ourselves into debt. We are the architects of our problems. And so, when we decide to consolidate our debts, we may start to think like we have done something to repair the problem. We feel we have achieved something, but the fact is that nothing has changed. The debt will still stand, and nothing shall have changed; we are the same.

Debt is a fundamental issue. It includes impatience, poor financial management, and impulse buying. To fix this problem, you have to review yourself further than the amount of debt. Consolidating the loans doesn't change anything; it is like transferring the problem from one party to another. If you want to see a permanent long-term change that will affect your future finances, then it is crucial to fix individual habits that led to the debt.

Just because everyone is doing it doesn't mean that you need to do it. The fact is that you don't need to get a credit card to grow your credit. Car loans aren't the ticket to a better life, and you can't repair your debt problem by consolidating it. By rejecting these lies and trying to live in a disciplined and responsible manner, you will prepare yourself for success and finally achieve complete financial freedom.

4. That you can declare bankruptcy

It is the last thought that many people often think about—that when the business fails, or your student loan debt grows beyond your abilities, bankruptcy is the last option. It is not the choice that most people want, but it is there as an exit route.

However, it's even hard to accomplish these responsibilities when you have declared bankruptcy. This is especially true when you have some reasonable household income.

The fact is that before you can file for bankruptcy, you have to fulfill several requirements before you are discharged for bankruptcy. Also, you may have to demonstrate that you are insolvent rather than able to pay off your debt after some time.

5. Debt advice is expensive

While certain debtors will ask you for some fee before giving you advice, many expert firms and organizations will offer advice free of charge. The consulting charities plus debt management firms can assist you in gaining knowledge of debt options.

6. Having debt is a bad thing

Despite the perception of debt, as a borrower, you need not be ashamed of borrowing, especially when you know you are doing it wisely. Mortgages will allow you to stay in a home that will probably increase in value, and student loans will provide you with methods to invest in yourself.

By choosing to use credit cards, you will get the chance to demonstrate that you can borrow responsibly, and pay all your bills on time, and by doing so, you will be increasing your credit score. A high credit score will also make financial organizations feel secure to lend you more money, and you may even qualify for big loan terms and attractive rates of interest.

Similarly, non-creditors, such as home insurers, electric utilities, landlords and cell phone companies, may also be interested to see your credit score. However, remember that when you constantly have a specific amount of credit card debt compared to your line amounts, it may negatively affect your credit score.

7. Maintaining a credit card balance will increase your credit score

This is another misconception. One way to improve your credit score is to use a small size of your credit, making sure that you pay all your bills on time every month.

8. Retail credit cards are a good thing

Not really. You need to read the part that talks about when you carry the balance of a previous month to the next month. The retail credit cards can be very attractive, especially when you are given free interest and rewards; however, when you carry the balance of this month into the next month, things start to fall apart fast. Some cards are similar to payment plans, where borrowers will buy a card from retailers, and then pay it after some months with "interest-free"; however, when you fail to clear the whole balance within the quoted period, you will perhaps pay interest on the entire amount, and at a higher interest rate than a normal credit card. For instance, Apple provides customers with an eighteen-month interest-free option when you use Barclaycard US card to make purchases. However, if you fail to pay off the purchase in the interest-free time, a variable yearly rate percentage is implemented. Your history isn't that important; whether you have a great credit history or not, you may easily find yourself paying an interest of 20%.

9. It is wise to throw away credit cards that you don't use

Probably not; in fact, you need to maintain old cards that have no balances and use them a little to ensure that they remain active. The reason extends to your credit score, and an aspect applied is computation, referred to as "credit utilization rate".

10. Once you are married, you are responsible for your spouse's debt

Most couples think that once they are married, the debts merge, but this is not the case. It is popular for couples to pay off debts together, but no spouse is bound to pay off the debt of his or her life partner.

There are methods in which security may be lost once they get married; however, you can be accountable for the debt your spouse applies if you include your name on the promissory note.

11. Debts are cleared after six years

Unfortunately, there is no way a debt can be cleared if you haven't paid it. Even if it is going to last ten years, the records will remain to show that you need to pay a specific amount for a given debt. This misconception tends to be propagated by graduates.

12. Consumer proposals are a bad thing to handle debt

This is yet another big misconception spread about debt. Well, consumer proposals have some drawbacks; however, they serve a certain purpose and are usually applied when debt rises to unmanageable heights.

And the reason why consumer proposals have bad perception is that personal finance bloggers usually hit out on them, simply because personal finance advocates living a debt-free life. However, a consumer proposal isn't meant for normal debt reduction. Consumer proposals assist people when they have a massive amount of debt. If living frugal and creating a budget doesn't reduce your debt, then consumer proposal could turn out to be the most reasonable choice.

They are also acceptable and legal to handle huge sums of debt and offer an alternative to bankruptcy. It is a minimum measure, and when structured in the right way, it can be a handy option. You need to know that handling debt becomes a problem when you have to come up with a plan to control your money and develop your credit rating.

13. Bankruptcy affects a credit score extensively such that you can't be approved for credit again.

Not true. If you are planning to file for bankruptcy, your credit score is already poor from the late payments and large amounts of debts. Declaring bankruptcy may not affect your score the way you think. Fair Isaac Corporation says that if you have a score of about 680, then bankruptcy may reduce it by 130-150 points. This is an approximation. It is hard to predict the exact effects. Even when your credit score drops, you may still qualify for a line of credit. Many lenders have stopped to consider bankruptcy as a deal breaker when they approve and deny credit applications. Bankruptcy can help free some of your salaries so that you can pay for future debts. Keep in mind too, that bankruptcy isn't permanent; it is removed from your credit report after seven to ten years.

14. Paying debts will immediately repair your credit report

False. A credit report will show you a summary of your current credit standing and your credit history. Much negative information remains on your credit report for either seven or more years. By clearing your debts, it will help increase your credit report and credit score, but it will not clear all past problems. It requires time.

15. You need to pay off the mortgage as fast as possible

This is false only when considered in a one-size-fits-all form. Mortgages have a massive debt, and clearing them away may remove a major factor of stress and financial problems, especially when you are close to retiring.

Rushing to pay off your mortgage isn't the right option for everyone. Some of the things that you need to think about include:

- Is it better to invest the money on additional payments?

- Are the tax benefits that come with the mortgage interest deduction significant to you?

- Will retiring your mortgage early imply that you need to sacrifice other crucial things, such as paying off your credit card balances every month?

16. You can budget away out of debt

There is a significant difference between the financial crisis and debt.

Many people with huge debts have probably overspent their income. Credit became a means to fulfill their lives. And today they have 30K in debt, and have to work hard, earn extra, and begin a debt snowball.

That said, there's a massive difference in the way you can overcome debt and the way you can go through a financial crisis. For certain individuals, the most comprehensive budget and extreme lifestyle cut may not solve the issue of income because it cannot fulfill the fixed costs and debts payments.

The fact is that debt can turn out to become a financial crisis, and this is where many people lack the experience to handle high amounts of debt.

This is the point where you find someone losing their home. This is the time when a lawsuit begins. This is where savings are cashed out, insurance payments come to a standstill, and bankruptcy comes to mind.

The good debt versus bad debt

Before you make that final step to borrow money, it is important to understand the difference between what is considered good debt and what is said to be bad debt. Some debts are worth it; others can infect you with a financial crisis.

Some people find it hard to live debt free—at least they will have some debt to pay off. While some debts are discouraged, good debt is considered as the money you borrow so that you can pay for things that you really need or things that increase in value. On the flip side, bad debt is one that arises from things that you only want and often decrease in value.

So that you can understand the difference between good debt and bad debt, you need to know the difference between wants and needs. Before you can borrow money, you have to decide whether the money is going to do something that will have a negative and positive effect on your general financial condition.

Of course, debt isn't a bad thing; it's just how you use the money that matters.

For a good debt, you will always have a good reason to justify it, and a developed plan for paying it so that you can clear the debt as quickly as possible.

An individual with good debt will also have the cheapest methods of borrowing money. They will do this by looking at the borrowing method, rate of interest, credit amount, and charges that are appropriate to them.

Sometimes, it may imply a deal with the least possible interest rate, but sometimes, it may not.

Examples of good debt

1. Paying for medical care

There is no fixed amount of money to borrow to ensure your loved one stays healthy. You can manage to pay off the money you borrow, but it is impossible to replace a human life. If a person requires expensive treatments to ensure they remain healthy, this would be an acceptable debt, no matter what.

2. Borrow money for education

When you apply for a student loan debt, you aren't making a wrong decision. In general, people with college degrees earn more income in their life than those without a degree.

And applying for a student loan so that you can support the education of your child defeats the idea of using your savings. After all, you cannot borrow money to pay for your savings. Multiple government programs provide low-interest student loans, and you can always cut student loan interest on your taxes.

3. Taking out a mortgage on a home

Taking a loan of this amount can be overwhelming, but purchasing a house creates ownership in something that will house you, and generate some retirement money. Even while you struggle to clear your debt, you may consider it an advantage to put any available liquid cash as a deposit, though it may not be the right choice.

A home mortgage interest is cut on your taxes, and the rate of interest is lower on your home loan than on the credit card. In other words, it is important to have money to pay for other expenses instead of credit.

Though purchasing a house was initially considered a strong, future-proof investment, certain homeowners do find themselves on the wrong side on their home mortgage loan. They owe banks more than the value of their homes. However, strategic planning, purchasing only what you can afford, and maintaining low interest by having good credit may allow you to purchase a home that one day you will own completely.

4. Buying a car

If you don't have public transport in your area, or you cannot manage to get someone with whom you can carpool with, then you may have to consider buying a car. An auto loan can either be "good" or "bad", but the main thing is to ensure that the auto loan is a good debt, so look for the lowest possible rates on your loan. In addition, you need to make a large down payment while ensuring that you remain with some cash on hand just in case you need it.

Your best goal should be to go for a used car model instead of a brand-new one, possibly saving yourself thousands on the sticker price and the interest that is paid throughout the loan.

5. Business loans

While this may not be seen as good debt, borrowing money to begin a business or expand a business is perhaps a great idea if the business is thriving. After all, you need money to make more money, right?

Sometimes, you may have to borrow capital to employ new people, purchase a new device, pay for advertisement, or even develop the first new widget you designed. The point is that you borrow this money to expand the business or increase income, then this will count as good debt.

What is bad debt?

Bad debt is that which depletes your wealth and isn't affordable. Plus, it provides no means to pay for itself.

Bad debts may have no realistic repayment plans and usually deplete when people buy things at an impulse. If you aren't sure whether you can repay the money, then don't borrow the money because that will be a bad debt.

Examples of bad debt

1. The credit card debt

A typical household in the United States has a balance of more than $10,000 on their credit card every month. However, the debt usually increases faster than we may realize and is always used to purchase things that we want instead of need. It is easier to think that you can afford something using a card than paying it with cash.

By the time you pay for your credit card, the interest rates of $100 items can be $200, and most items depreciate quickly—this makes the loss significant. In other words, credit card debt is a form of bad debt and one in which millions of Americans are using today. It is tough to pay off your credit card debt, and that is why it is better to avoid it in the first place.

2. Borrowing from a 401K

When you ask for money from a 401K program, you will need to chat with the IRS, and if you aren't using the money to purchase a home, you will need to pay the loan in five years. If you fail to pay it back, you risk being charged with a severe penalty. Also, the interest that you pay on the loan will get taxed twice.

You can't get a loan to fund your retirement. For that reason, borrowing money from your retirement plan to use it to pay for anything that isn't part of retirement is a bad idea. You will be putting your retirement at risk when you get a loan from a 401k, so don't make this mistake.

3. Payday loans

It may appear easy to borrow money from payday loan firms, but it is hard to pay it back. These companies offer loans with very high interest rates. The companies take advantage of the fact that many people need that money. As a result, borrowing a small amount may end up costing you a lot.

Payday loans aren't considered the worst kind of debt that you can take on. If you really need a short-term loan, it is better to go for a cash advance on a credit card rather than borrow money from these firms.

4. Jewelry, expensive clothes, and vacations

If you can't afford to pay for these luxuries using real cash, then don't do it. These are not needs but wants, and that means they are bad debt. Wait until the time when you have money to pay for them. By running into debt so that you can go for a vacation is perhaps a terrible use of money.

In summary, modern life demands many of us to borrow money at one point; however, learning the difference between good debt and bad debt can make a huge difference in your financial health and opportunity for success.

It is better not to get into more debt that you will struggle to pay back, whether it is good or bad. In addition, don't let debt accrue to more than 36% of your total gross income because credit agencies can't distinguish between a good and bad debt when calculating your credit score. If you find yourself having many debts, then you will need to search for ways to reduce your debt and get back on track.

Don't let debt scare you; instead, use it as a means to improve your life or financial condition, invest in your future, or increase your earnings.

Steps to pay back your debts fast

Paying off all your debt isn't easy, but it is possible, even if you have the least amount of money, no properties, and no idea of how to begin. Whether you are struggling with credit cards or mortgage loans, these steps will help you get out of debt fast, regardless of whether you are dead broke:

ep 1: Know how much debt you need to pay back

You may not believe the amount of money people throw away by skipping this first step and paying bills blindly without taking a more in-depth look.

This narrows down to the fact that people have a negative attitude towards debt. They consider debt as a big crime and shame in their life. And so, they feel guilty about their debt. When feeling this way, you will never want to think about how much debt you need to pay; in fact, some prefer to bury their heads in the sand than confront the reality of the situation.

This is basically what credit and loan companies look forward to. They want to hide from you the statement, and then you send them the minimum payment knowing that you have cleared all your debt. They enjoy it when you do it that way.

What you need to learn today is that the minimum payments drain your pocket more.

It can be hurtful to learn the truth by yourself, but you have to swallow the pill. From this point, you can learn that it is not hard to avoid this habit; in fact, credit card companies can assist you. Find your credit card and call the number at the back, and ask them for the debt you owe, the APR, and minimum monthly payment.

This is the time to step up and accept your debt. You either choose to do the hard work now or suffer doing the impossible later.

Luckily, this chart will help you achieve that.

How much debt do you have?

Name of credit card	The total amount of debt	APR	Monthly minimum payment

This table will help you know how much you need to pay for every company, and the interest rates.

Now stop and do this.

Have you done so?

Congratulations! Implementing the first step is always the most challenging. Now you are on your way to becoming debt free.

If the total number of debt appears high, consider the following things:

1. There are many people with more debt than you.

2. From today that number is going to reduce. This is the start of the end.

Now that you know how much you owe, what next?

Step 2: Chose your "strategy of attack" for clearing the debt

Once you know the exact amount of debt, you are ready to begin working on your debt. To achieve this, you have to organize the type of debts you're going to pay first. Whether you want to pay student loans, a credit card—whatever depending on your choice.

To fully pay off all your debt, you may have to start with the loan that has the highest interest rate.

For instance, assume credit card A has a balance of $1,000 and a 12% interest rate, whereas credit card B has $1,500 and 6% interest. You channel $150 per month by paying the minimum payment (3%) on one and the remaining amount on the other. This means you will save a lot of money by clearing credit card A ($147 interest) compared to card B ($188).

When you decide what you want to start with first, the next thing is to develop the plan of attack.

For student loans, you can probably save thousands of dollars every year, and pay down your debt more each month.

Yes. You can save money by spending MORE.

Assume you have $10,000 as a student loan, and the interest rate is 6.8 %, with a ten-year period to complete the payment.

If you apply the standard monthly plan, you will have to pay $115 per month.

But can you find out how much you can save every year if you simply paid $100 more every month?

Monthly payments	Total interest paid	You save
$115	$3,810	$0
$215	$1,640	$2,169
$315	$1,056	$2,754
$415	$782	$3,027

As mentioned, paying the least amount is more expensive. Even $30 per month can save you lots of money.

Step 3: Time to freeze your credit card debt—to stop it from growing

If you ever wanted to pay off all your debts, you have to learn to reduce your debt. That is the reason why this step requires you to implement these things:

1. Find your wallet.

2. Get all your credit cards.

3. Send them by mail to a different location.

Well, perhaps you don't need to go this extreme… but this makes you see the main point, which is to eliminate all temptation of wanting to use the credit card/s. You can only think of using it once you are debt free.

Here is a great tip that may work for you: throw all your cards into a basin of water and plunge them all into your freezer. If you can freeze your credit, you may need to insert your hands through a huge block of ice for you to get it back. This provides you with the time to decide whether or not you want the thing that you planned to buy.

Similarly, you can put all your credit cards in a safe, or whomever you trust to keep them for you. The point is that you aren't supposed to increase your credit card debt.

Step 4: Use this template to negotiate

Many people aren't aware of this, but it can help you save more than $900 in interest if you learn tips of negotiation.

Using negotiation tips, you can manage to limit the APR on your credit card and generate thousands of bucks.

Step 5: Make use of your "hidden income" to pay off your extra $1,000 + /month

If you have come to this point, you could be saying, "This is nice and all, but where do I find the money to pay the bills?"

Here are four recommended things:

1. Utilize the cash you have made from Step 4.

2. Make use of the money you have earned from a Conscious Spending Plan.

3. Get deeper into hidden income.

4. Earn a lot of money.

Secrets to getting out of debt

Debt can bog you down and makes it difficult for a person to live a great life. If you are tired of struggling to pay your debt, here are some secrets to help you get out of debt:

1. Daydreaming can assist you to get out of debt

Daydreaming is a great way to come out of debt. Obviously, you don't want to spend your entire time fantasizing, but if you can spend some minutes imagining your credit card balance/s at zero, it can do wonders.

Mindful meditation can help reduce your blood pressure and allow you to develop a positive mindset about clearing debt; this can be useful in taking the right action.

2. Say no to late charges—and this will increase your opportunities of getting out of debt

The amount of cash that is pumped into the late charges can damage your efforts to clear your debt. If possible, you can put an end to paying late fees. If maintaining a track of when your bills will be due is hard, then you need to consider using an app such as Check, which will notify you when it is the correct time to pay.

3. Confirm your balances every day

This may appear to be overkill, but it's not. Quick reminders should be your best bet to get out of debt. If you only check your balances once per month when you pay your bills, after a few days, the truth of your debt may start to disappear in your mind. Then when a spending chance comes up, you are likely to bite and drive yourself into more debt.

Every day when you rise, take the time to review your debt condition. By seeing it the way it is, you will be encouraged to stick to your budget, and look at your debt getting cleared.

4. Declare your plans to get out of debt

Talk to your friends and family about your plans for clearing the debt. Tell them to keep on asking about your debt.

5. Plan to become a one-car household

If you have two cars, plan on eliminating one and walk while you go to work or carpool. You may be surprised to learn that these little habits can save you thousands every year by using a single car. The average vehicle owner does spend more than $9,000 annually to maintain their vehicle.

6. Have two jobs to help pay down your debt fast

Finding a second job, or regularly selecting an extra shift or two, is a quick way for people to clear their debt; however, this strategy doesn't apply to everyone, but if you can succeed to make it work, you may free yourself from debt within a few years. For this to occur, you need to use all your additional income to pay your debt. Working extra hours doesn't have to be permanent—once you have cleared your debts, you can consider scaling back again.

You can also think about building an extra income to clear your debt by taking advantage of a hobby you like, or even a skill set that you like. For instance, if you know how to write, you can try out freelancing for newspapers, media outlets, and blogs on freelance sites. If you enjoy crafting, you can think about selling your work on Etsy. If you are good at handy work, you may look for a site which will help you link up with people who require extra skills.

Some people even use their homes to make extra cash. Can it be possible for you also to rent your storage space in your garage, or even rent your house on Airbnb?

7. Refinancing your mortgage

If you have a mortgage, you might have sufficient equity to merge all your mortgage debts. If you don't have enough equity in your house, extra mortgage costs may be expensive. Just ensure that you review all the options and look for advice from a different person besides your lender. If a normal bank isn't enough to assist you, don't be quick to look for the first home equity finance firm that is ready to provide you money. However, you should engage in a conversation with a certified, non-profit credit counselor first. You might have great options apart from refinancing your house that you aren't aware of. They can assist you in reviewing all the options available and developing the best plan to drive you forwards and fulfill your financial goals.

If you succeed in refinancing your house and merge debts into your mortgage, you may have to start thinking of a new mortgage. It is very important that you ensure your spending is within your income. Having a budget that you follow is the best way to do this and assign cash to every monthly saving. If you fail to save money, you could be tempted to ask for more when "emergencies" emerge.

8. Avoid paying retail

Make it your goal to get out of debt and avoid paying a complete price. Always go for a bargain for all your purchases, and if you don't get a deal on brand names, generics are another option.

You can save huge income that can be channeled to clearing debt by asking price comparisons, shopping sales, and store coupons that are found through smartphone apps.

9. Have accounts at two different banks

Divide and conquer works magically when you want to pay off your debt. Allocate enough money into your daily checking account to deal with daily and monthly expenses. Get a different account to contribute your debt money, like an online bank.

Avoid carrying the debit card for a debt account so that you don't use the money for daily purchases. Pay off your debt from that account alone.

Using the law of attraction to come out of debt

If you positively think about becoming debt free, then the "law of attraction" can help you realize your goals. You may be asking yourself whether you only need to think positively as the only method to pay off your debt, or even asking whether the law of attraction is a practical means to avoid debt accumulation?

Whether this is going to be your first encounter with the law of attraction, or you have been practicing it before, the secret is that it will help you develop the right mindset to become debt free.

Keep in mind that everything in the world is energy. Each element in the world has its unique vibrational energy. Humans have a vibrational frequency, money has a vibrational frequency, and even debt has a vibrational frequency. While you match the vibrational frequency of objects, you will be drawing them nearer to you.

If you have debt, then you have to match the vibrational frequency of the debt. You may still need to change the vibrational frequency so that it can be the same with being debt free, and match the money frequency.

How to change your vibrational frequency

1. The thoughts

There is a high probability that you spend a good amount of time thinking about the debt you have. You could be wondering how and when you will manage to clear it. This is the worst thing to do because you will be drawing a lot of debt to you. Every time these thoughts come to you, you will be changing your vibration to the one of being in debt.

All your thoughts are normally self-fulfilling. The process of thinking you are in debt results in you applying the law of attraction to stay in debt.

Stop concentrating on debt, and begin thinking about what you want to attain—financial security, freedom, excellent credit, and sufficient money to buy whatever you want.

You also need to stop concentrating on the debt that you have because it can discourage you.

2. Your feelings

Did you know that your feelings can create?

Yes, your feelings can show what you are building in life at any time. Your feelings will allow you to implement the law of attraction to come out of debt.

When feeling good, you will be on your way to becoming debt free. A lot of money and opportunities will come to you to pay off the debt.

You can't assume that you'll feel better once you become debt free. You need to feel good at this moment so that the law of attraction can relieve you from debt. First, feel good, and things will become better.

When you are overwhelmed or even disappointed, you can see all kinds of problems. When you feel happy, joyful, and uplifted, you will see the opportunities and steps you can make to change your debt.

3. Heart energy

This is a powerful method to use to get out of debt fast. The method requires you to send heart energy to every individual you owe money to.

Send it to every person who works at your credit card company and bank.

Send it to every person at the store when you buy clothing, groceries, and much more.

Look at each bill that is brought to you because you are surrounded by heart energy.

The most important thing is to send the heart energy to money that comes to you. It will attract money to you like a magnet.

4. Celebrate

This is the time to start celebrating when you make it. Whether it is jumping up and down in happiness, or even thanking yourself, enjoy that your debt is paid off.

Enjoy the little success that you experience as you pay off each debt, and start to get your head above water.

You will be changing your vibration to one where you are debt free every time you do so. It is simple to apply the law of attraction to jump out of debt.

Where to find money

If you struggle to clear your credit card balances, you may have to consider alternative ways—if possible, a side hustle to make some extra cash. If you don't know places that you can turn to for extra income, don't worry: you can make money online using the least amount of effort.

Let's look at some of the methods you can apply to make money online:

1. Mechanical Turk

If you want to generate some money doing little tasks, Mechanical Turk can be the best way to go. Amazon powers this site, and it allows clients to post simple tasks with short instructions, including transcriptions, surveys, audio recordings, and many more. Most of these tasks pay a little amount of cash, but the task is easy to complete. Plus, it takes a short time, and the sign-up process is quick and easy.

2. eBay

This is a great site to make some passive income. Here, you can sell anything that you want, and generate some extra money to pay your debts. It doesn't need much effort; you simply get products or even create products that you believe people will enjoy purchasing. Once you have ideas about the things you want to sell, you will realize that you can make more cash, and pay all your monthly bills.

3. Swagbucks

For Swagbucks, you get the chance to earn money doing what you perhaps spend many hours doing browsing the internet. If you create a Swagbucks account, you will receive points for doing simple tasks like shopping online, watching popular videos, and completing surveys within the app. Once you have accumulated enough Swagbucks, you can move on to redeem the points into cash. This is an easy method to convert your everyday browsing habits into a means of earning money to clear your credit card debt fast.

4. Ibotta

While you may focus on paying off debts on your credit cards, you will still need to eat and purchase things. Ibotta can assist you in changing your shopping trips into easy money and paying off your debts. The app will provide you with thousands of rebates for items commonly bought; you only buy an item, scan the receipt and the barcode of the item into your smartphone, and let Ibotta credit your account with the rebate. Once you make $20 or more, you can transfer the money into your PayPal or bank account. This app has different features that will allow you to make extra cash every month, and you will always offer cash rebates to scan a grocery receipt into the app.

5. HQ Trivia

Making some extra cash online is a bit easy, especially when you get an account with HQ Trivia. This is a big online game. When you create an account and play, you will make money for answering the trivia questions of the game correctly. While you accumulate cash in the game, you can easily transfer that to your PayPal account.

6. Acorns

Acorn is a micro-investing firm that builds an investment account for you. This account will link you to one or even more credit cards. Once you buy using the credit card, Acorn will round it up to the nearest dollar and transfer the amount to your investment account. The money that Acorn invests differs depending on the investment risk you want to take. With time, you can accrue a specific value in your Acorns account and ensure you pay off all your debts.

7. Craigslist

This site features "jobs and gigs" where you can find multiple methods to make additional money to pay off debt. You will do everything from odd jobs around the house to tasks that need specific skills like nursing, software engineering, and real estate.

Still, you can use it with other methods to get tutoring work, and so forth.

How much should you pay off towards your debts?

Everyone hates to be in debt, but the fact is that nearly everyone has some debt. Your target should be to have the least amount of debt as possible so that you can save and remain with a lot of cash. The challenge is how to arrive there. You must have realistic expectations and discipline. You can experience peace of mind in that you are in great shape.

Suggestions are quite different on the amount of debt a person has to have and finding your perfect state may take time if you have a big debt. Recommendations on the amount of income that should be directed towards bills and debt will provide you with the groundwork to take control of your debts.

The net income budget

To have a clear picture of the amount of money you need to spend, you should apply your after-tax or net income to decide the percentage that should be directed towards your debts. According to Liz Weston, a personal finance guru for MSN money, individuals reserve 50% of their net income for needs in life, including mortgages, rent, utilities, transportation, and minimum payments on credit cards and loans. Then, 30% of the income is directed to entertainment and other requirements of Weston's budget plan. The other 20% is directed to savings, extra payments, retirement funds, and payments to reduce the percentage of debts.

The debt-to-income ratio

If you go to the bank and request a loan, one of the first things they will want to look before they can grant you the loan is your "debt-to-income ratio". Banks require that your monthly debt payments should not be more than 36% of your gross monthly income. Typically, it has to be about 10%, but if it's lower than 20%, you are still in a good state. In other words, the money you are going to pay out each month for the mortgage, including payments of a credit card, taxes and insurance should not exceed 36%. Before you can start to feel scared, keep in mind that the computation is on your gross income and not the money you take home. The remaining amount has to account for utilities, living expenses, entertainment, clothes, and food.

Mortgage debt

Your monthly mortgage, including your taxes and insurance, has to be over 28% of your monthly gross income. This means, if you earn $4,000 per month, your monthly mortgage debt shouldn't be more than $1,440.

Credit card debt

Unless you make a plan to pay off your credit card debts at the end of every month, they can be a huge problem in your finances. But you will have to stand up and take it. Clear the debts as soon as you can. Once you pay, make sure that you only charge what you can manage to pay full when the statement arrives. This is the reason: the interest that is charged on credit cards is high, and all the money you are paying on interest can be used elsewhere for something important.

Other suggestions

According to the SmartMoney site, the U.S Federal Reserve Board considers a person to be in a financial crisis if the debt obligations are more than 40% of the gross income; however, the website also warns those with a debt of more than 30%. The website says that you may only have 20% of your income to account for taxes when 25% is consumed in debts.

Since the advice on debt management is different from person to person, it is usually hard to know how much of your salary should go toward clearing your debt/s. However, the ultimate thing is to assist you in continuing to reduce your debt and increase your savings. As a result, the best technique recommended is to choose a plan that you are likely to stick with and measure your success using that plan after several months. Adjust the plan as much as you need to in order to cut down your debt/s and increase your savings.

Creating a debt pay off plan that you can stick with

If you want to clear all your debts, you must know how to create a great debt pay off plan, which you can stick with. Here is a step-by-step guide to help you clear your debts:

Know your why

By far, this is the most crucial step, and it doesn't only apply in paying debts but also many other things you want to accomplish in life. In the book *The 7 Habits of Highly Effective People* by Steven Covey, this step is discussed.

The goals you set in life allow you to prioritize many things. Giving yourself time to come up with reasons to explain why you are doing something makes it easier to stick with. Most importantly, something that needs much self-control, such as paying off debt. Maintaining your why in mind will grant you the ability to overcome the different challenges. Additionally, it will assist you in building a debt pay off plan that comprises of your entire goals.

Learning your why and developing an image of what you want to attain and be in life is the main aspect of nurturing good new habits and upholding them.

Depending on your why you may decide to pay all your debts at once, and once you have paid all your debts, make a decision not to accumulate any other debt. Keep in mind that it is impossible to get out of debt if you continue to overspend.

Understand all your debts

Before you can start to create your debt paying approach, you need to understand what you are working with. Start by building a list of all the debts that you owe. This should include all your credit cards, student loans, etc.

Next to every item, write the interest rate, current balance, minimum payment due, and the expected payment date—this date is important to remind you how much longer you have before it expires.

Now that you have an overview of what your debts are, you can come up with a strong decision about your plans with the debt. Depending on your set goals, you may decide to pay some of your debts slowly so that you have enough flexibility.

Build a realistic budget

So far, you know much about your debts; it is time to take a look at your current expenditure in life. This means you must have a budget. Luckily, you have one.

Your budget should include your current living expenditure, such as groceries, car maintenance, and clothing—also include dog food, gifts, and so forth.

When the budget is realistic, you are likely to stick with it, and this will benefit your debt repayment plan. Consider it this way: if you know the amount of money you spend and you choose not to spend in certain areas for the next six months, you will save yourself a lot of money.

When you trim your budget, you save money, which you can then use to pay your debt. In other words, having a realistic budget and sticking with it will highly benefit you in the long run.

Determine the amount you are left with to pay off your debt

At this stage, you already know how your debt appears, and you know the extra cash you have to channel it towards payment of the debt.

Make a quick decision of how fast you want to clear your debt

At this point, you have everything to help you decide what you need to do to pay off your debt. You can decide not to change anything about your current lifestyle and simply clear your debt based on the extra money your budget allows you to have. On the flipside, you may decide to trim your budget and apply for a side job so that you can make extra income to pay off the debt.

The real answer to how fast you want to clear all your debts depends on how fast you want to realize your financial and life goals.

Decide which debts you want to finish first

There are two popular methods used in debt repayment:

"Snowball", where you pay debts beginning with the smallest. The concept behind this method is that small wins will rejuvenate you to continue paying your debts; and

"Debt avalanche", where you have to pay off your debt beginning with the highest interest debts then moving down to the lowest. The advantage of this method is that you will end up paying less interest as time goes on.

Automate your finances

Since you have your debt payment strategy in place, you will want to make it as easy for yourself as possible. One way of doing this is by automating your finances.

Your expenditure should comprise of enough money to deal with your monthly bills; this should comprise of the extra amount you direct towards debts. The account you use to buy things should be linked to the debit card that you apply to your discretionary purchases, such as gas and food.

If you can, let your employer divide your paycheck before it is deposited into your account. If an employer fails to provide you with the option, implement an automatic transfer through your bank.

By applying a hands-off technique to your debt pay off plan, it begins to decrease every month. Your goals will be realized while you concentrate on your day-to-day activities. You will still need to look at your bills and budget to ensure that you remain on track.

Four ways to protect yourself from the unexpected

Don't give room to unexpected expenses to damage your financial plans.

When it comes to unexpected expenses, such as medical bills and car repairs, many of us are always unprepared. And when a financial crisis such as a job loss becomes severe, the less prepared many of us are. According to a study conducted by Pew Charitable Trusts in 2015, half of Americans aren't ready for a financial crisis or unexpected event. Another study by Pew found out that 55% of American homes don't have cash savings to cater for an income of one month. While being scared of the unexpected will keep you awake at night, here are some steps to implement to secure your finances:

1. Understand the condition of your current finances

It is impossible to plan your finances when you don't have a clear understanding of your income and spending. First, you need to define your average monthly income, including any additional money you make. Then outline your average monthly spending; this should comprise of everything—your student loan, car repayment, entertainment, and hobbies. If your income is higher than your expenses, the difference is what you can save for the unexpected. In case your expenses are higher than your income, then you will have to examine your finances and identify methods to cut down on your spending.

2. Set up an emergency debt

Once you develop a clear picture of your finances, then you can compute the least that you require each month to handle your expenses. You can begin by prioritizing your bills. Examine your costs and outline your monthly bills. These are bills that you have to pay every month, such as the mortgage, groceries, utilities, and many more. Next, you should outline your optional expenditures; for example, a gym membership, eating, TV, and Netflix. The total amount of your necessities is what you require each month.

Assess your optional expenditure and find out whether there is something you can reduce. Instead of going out every day to eat, you can change and apply a different option. If you can understand these and many other debt myths, you will gain the confidence to make better financial decisions today that may impact you in the future.

Chapter 3: Saving Money

All of us have strong reasons when it comes to saving money. We like to say that we will begin to save once we attain a specific milestone; for example, when we reach a certain age or get a salary increment, or when children move out.

However, the truth is that you can only begin to save when you build healthy money habits and your future needs are more critical than your wants.

Don't be scared; it is not as hard as it looks. With some changes to your methods of spending, you'll be on the right track to save money.

Why don't many Americans save money?

Everyone knows that they need to save some money for every income they earn, but many people don't save with the knowledge that they are supposed to save. According to a report published by the Federal Reserve, approximately 40% of Americans have the challenge to cover a $400 emergency. The reason is that they have competing goals.

In most cases, the purpose of saving money isn't a big enough priority to slow down buying a new smartphone, TV, or kitchen table. In other words, most people spend their money or get into debt to purchase the latest want. This debt then becomes a monthly payment that may affect paychecks and lives.

Well, what is the goal of saving money?

You can eliminate the habit of living on a paycheck by applying a simple secret: create a zero-based budget before the month starts. A budget requires a person to become intentional. It assists a person in building a plan and identifying where the money is flowing and how much you can save every month. It is never too late to take control of your money.

Reasons why you should consider saving money

Now that credit is very easy to get, you may ask why a person may prefer to save money and make a purchase with real cash. If you want a certain product, you remove your credit card and pay it using a debit card. However, if you know that you can manage to pay the credit at the end of the month, what's the problem? It is unfortunate that many people are buying into this idea. Below are some of the reasons why you need to save:

1. To become independent financially

The metrics for becoming wealthy are based on whom you talk to. Being economically independent may refer to the ability to go on a vacation any time you want, abandoning work and returning to school to change careers, or even investing in another person's start-up. This may also mean taking a lesser job that you feel satisfied with financially, or retiring when you want to instead of working because you have no choice otherwise.

Financial independence is different from being rich. Having savings that you can depend on is what shows how "rich" you are regardless of how you define it.

2. Save 50% on anything you purchase

If you use your credit to purchase products and delay to pay for the credit at the end of the month, then you are perhaps paying higher interest for the lateness. It is important to stop relying on credit cards if you want to save up. Savings will allow you to buy items when they are put on sale and spend time on making better decisions. When you buy products using real money, you tend to save about 50% of what you could have paid as interest to credit card companies.

3. Purchase a car

Before you can buy a new car, you have to make a down payment first to help you get an affordable interest rate. While you can get this money from your credit card, the interest charged is a bit high. However, when you save some money, you can use it to make a down payment that will allow you to reduce the interest that you will have to pay.

4. Purchase a home

It is hard for a bank to offer you some cash to buy a house if you don't pay some down payment, and you aren't allowed to borrow a down payment. You need to have this money kept, saved, or have a person assist you with but not lend you. A down payment should be about 5% of the buying price of the house, and then the bank will decide whether to lend you the remaining 95%. There are different costs and fees that you are required to pay when you purchase a home; that means you need an extra 5% for those expenditures.

5. Emergencies

Though we remain optimistic that emergencies will not arise, the truth is that they do happen. A family member might develop a health problem that may require an emergency trip to the hospital, or an accident may occur, or bad weather may flood and crack pipes, or you may have to take a flight to attend the funeral of a loved one. These kinds of emergencies are quite expensive; that is the reason why it's important to be prepared.

6. You can lose your job

When having good moments, everyone believes that their job is protected, but on bad days, many start to understand that evil things can occur to anyone. You can wake up and lose your job or even experience an accident. Employment Insurance (EI) starts to hit you after six weeks. That is the reason why you need to have some savings. If you don't have any savings, you will have to use a credit card which is going to be more expensive.

7. To have a better life

There are a lot of emotional, physical, and psychological effects that occur when you live a stressful life.

There is some truth to the saying that happiness also comes from being organized. There's much in your future that doesn't apply to your spending, but simply become organized and be in charge of your future.

8. Unforeseen expenses

What will you do in case your car requires significant repairs? Are you capable of raising $500-$3,000 instantly? Suppose your house needs a major renovation? You can look forward to the bank giving you some cash for all these things.

Don't wait for anything; start today by putting aside a little money every time you get paid until you have an emergency saving fund of between $500-$1000.

How to make money while sleeping?

You can save tons of money in your daily life from negotiating bills to limiting your spending. Even while you are asleep, saving money shouldn't stop.

Turn plugs off

Besides the fridge, freezer, and alarm clock, there's nothing you need to leave plugged in overnight. Before you head to the land of slumber, take a quick look around and ensure everything is switched off or unplugged.

Make this your nighttime routine. Walk from room to room to ensure that the kettle, microwave, toaster, DVD player, and TV are off.

It may not look like a big saving, but over the year, it will add up.

No opportunity to shop

Everyone has done this. Late in the evening, when there seems to be nothing on the television, you start to browse on the internet and view your favorite online shops. It is during this time that you order those pair of jeans, book a holiday and many other things.

If there is nothing on television, or you have nothing to do, go to bed early. If you are sound asleep, you will have no means to spend money, and you will protect your money from unnecessary spending.

Look at the taps

Have you ever been resting in bed when you heard the sound of a dripping tap in your house? Instead of continuing to enjoy your sleep, get up and sort it out. Not only is the sound of a dripping tap very annoying but it is also like throwing money down the drain.

Once you switch off the tap, you can sleep quietly without any distractions while knowing that your water bills won't be affected.

You will eat little

When you have a great night's sleep, not only will you feel refreshed in the morning, but it will help you to eat effectively. In other words, a better night's sleep will allow you to save money on the cost of food.

A research done by the University of Chicago discovered that subjects who decided to sleep for only four hours for two nights had an 18% drop in leptin, a hormone that sends the signal to the brain that there is no more food, and a 28% increase in ghrelin, a hormone that activates hunger.

In other words, enough sleep results in eating less food.

The myth of financial advisors

When you consider the idea of a "financial advisor", do you imagine a rich person resting in a posh office? Many people do, and rich people tend to employ financial advisors to help them manage their finances. However, financial advisors aren't meant for the rich alone.

If you aren't wealthy, you may think that you are doing everything fine to manage your finances, including saving each month and setting aside money for your retirement plan. This is a great start; however, that isn't enough. Having a professional may become critical if you don't have much cash to work with.

Experienced portfolio managers and retired officers can assist you to save and invest money. Maybe it is time to think about listening to what experts say.

There are just moments in life when you need an expert. Maybe you inherited a large sum of cash, or you received a settlement of a certain size. You may even have won the lottery. You understand managing a huge sum of cash isn't meant for amateurs. What about if all that comes to your bank account is your paycheck? Do you need a financial expert? Perhaps you should ask yourself the following questions:

- Do you have children about to go to college?

- Are you planning to get married soon, or are you recently divorced?

- Would you prefer to begin a business?

- Do you plan to retire at a certain point?

- Do you feel anxious about your financial future?

If you said "yes" to any of the above questions, consider looking for help.

The ten myths about financial advisors

Wall Street has a sophisticated marketing style that will persuade you to purchase their products, financial advice, and services. One technique is to take control of your assets.

There are facts and myths. As you are going to see, the myths generate substantial risk when you choose financial advisors and implement their advice. The more you are aware of myths, the more prepared you will be to secure your financial interests:

1. Financial advisors, sales representatives, and planners are all the same

This is simply not true. There is a big difference in quality-based services, education, certifications, compliance records, conflicts of interest, and other essential considerations. This difference builds a significant financial risk when you choose an advisor.

2. Experts must have the least amount of experience before they can deliver financial advice

The reality is that there are no minimum experience requirements for advisors. They can start selling financial services and products on the same day they get their licenses.

3. Advisors should have a college degree

There is no minimum education qualification for advisors.

4. Advisors should have a clean record of compliance to sell financial services, products, and advice.

A financial advisor can have numerous complaints on their records and still get the current licenses.

5. There are minimum requirements to refer yourself as a financial planner

This is also not true; anyone can become a financial planner regardless of whether they have the required experience or not.

6. Advisors working for main companies have safer choices than those who work for smaller companies

Big companies pay billions of dollars as a penalty for deceiving investors. Big companies have multiple, hidden conflicts of interest.

7. Advisors who receive compensation with commissions offer "free" advice and services

There is nothing like free advice and free services. Advisors receive commissions to sell investment and insurance products. The companies that generate products set the fees that they charge, or add deferred sales charges to compensate for the commissions they receive.

8. Older financial experts have more experience than young advisors

Wall Street companies assume that old advisors have more experience. As a result, they look for older advisors to build the notion of experience. This is the wrong sales practice.

Wealth management isn't just for the rich

Investing and management of wealth isn't meant for people such as Robert Kuok, who is considered among the richest people in Malaysia with assets worth USD 12 billion. It is important for middle-aged individuals to plan for retirement, and young couples to prepare for the education of their children.

Typically, wealthy management involves a mix of investment and financial planning. Investment refers to the practice of converting proportional investments into bonds, which involve security selection, asset mix selection, and monitoring.

On the other hand, financial planning describes the science of arranging economic issues, such as expenses, wills, estate planning, insurance, and lending. Both have a similar goal of realizing personal objectives.

With the purpose to accrue and preserve, wealth experts implement a financial plan based on the needs of the individual. As a result, it is reasonable to include all aspects of financial needs and status to build an efficient money management structure.

When done correctly, one can reduce the risks in investment, unnecessary expenses, taxes, and improving financial returns and boosting assets. It is necessary for enabling efficient use of assets during the lifetime of a person and transfer of assets at the time of death.

Why isn't the management of wealth just for the rich?

Managing your cash allows you to understand the way you can invest and save to fulfill different financial goals. This will help you to preserve wealth and control your expenses.

Sustainable retirement

Everyone should have a plan for retirement whether they are working in the public sector or self-employed. Based on a survey conducted by the Ministry of Human resources, about 14% of retirees finish their savings within the first three years of retirement, 5% within five years, and 70% within ten years.

To enjoy your retirement, you need to have sufficient savings to take care of your expenses and generate streams of passive income.

An expert in wealth management will advise you on the best methods for saving up for your future. If you aren't enrolled in the pension, you can begin to save for your retirement by using a private retirement scheme.

Save for your children's education

There is no bigger gift than educating your kids. The cost of education can be a bit high at private colleges, and so you need to have some savings.

For you to save and make sufficient money to cater for the education needs of your children, you are required to consider various investments that will suit their needs and risk tolerance. A wealth manager will recommend the best plan of action. Some of the available opportunities include capital financing, unit trusts, and bonds.

Those who don't mind the risk can invest in gold, commodities, and FOREX. These investments feature a big risk, but they can deliver significant long-term returns to investors.

Ensure that your family is secure financially

Insurance plays a big role in financial planning. It is essential to have enough insurance coverage to make sure that your family is financially secure against emergencies. Depending on the needs, it is possible to invest in medical insurance, life insurance, and many other options.

The goal isn't just to find insurance coverage but to look for sufficient coverage. With the right management in place, an individual may be aware of the total insured that is sufficient depending on the affordability and commitments.

Making sure that your wealth is passed on smoothly

Wealth management, when handled in the right way, can increase your money and assets. As a result, it is important to make sure that assets are assigned to the right persons if anything bad was to go wrong.

Highlight your investment beneficiaries to make sure that hard-earned investments go to your loved ones with the least legal formalities. It will be a time of grief, and it won't be okay to put them through the challenge of organizing the finances.

Control your short-term goals

You probably have short-term goals, such as purchasing a car, saving for a down payment on a house, or even furnishing the new home. To achieve these goals, you want to think about share financing and fixed deposits, as they deliver high liquidity and have a lower risk based on the short timeline.

A balanced wealth management system should include long-term and short-term goals before generating an effective plan to fulfill all the objectives based on the current potential.

It's for everyone

This means that money management plays a key role in achieving personal and financial dreams by implementing a diverse approach, which allows us to make plans for a better set of opportunities and risks.

Automatic Investing

Automatic investing is when you agree for a fixed amount of money to be cut from your paycheck every month and spent in a pre-determined allocation. The contribution that goes to the retirement plan is a great example. If your employer withdraws some cash from your paycheck every month and invests in the 401K, then you have automated your investment.

How can you automate investing?

This is a simple process. The first thing is to decide the amount of money you want to save and from which account. The next thing is to get in touch with your investment provider and let them be aware that you want to create an automatic investment strategy and how you want to invest the money.

Why Automatic Investing is a great idea

1. It's hard to spend the money

When you draft money automatically into your investment account, that means you can't get tempted to spend it. This will reduce discretionary spending and allow you to fulfill your financial goals.

2. *Fewer arguments*

Once your investment is automated, it is then possible to automate your savings, and that offers minimum room to fight for the amount to spend and is money kept for your future without any work. In other words, you don't need to convince your other partner of retirement planning.

3. *No work is needed*

It requires the least amount of effort to set up. Once everything is okay, your financial success will deal with everything. You will not waste time calling, being worried, and moving around. The money will be invested as you focus on other important things.

4. *The odds are in your favor*

Many people have their savings and investments in their retirement plans. There are two main explanations for this: first, tax penalties make it hard and expensive to use the money; secondly, the money will increase fast every month because you will be adding each month.

Though you can use your non-retirement account without suffering tax penalties, many people don't touch the automated accounts; they leave them to grow. Automating your investment is very simple, and the payoff is immense. It has additional benefits of securing your future, reducing your current spending, and cutting down your financial friction at home.

Building a smart investment portfolio

Many investors want to build investments that will deliver growth and income that is required to fulfill financial goals. To achieve that, you have to understand yourself as an investor. And the reason for this is that a portfolio that is good for someone else may not work for you. Below are some of the factors that you need to consider when building a smart investment portfolio:

- Your goals

- Your age

- The time for your different goals

- Your attitude towards risk

You also need to master ideas related to asset allocation. After this, you can begin to look into your investment selections and how different types of investments utilize your money. Your ability to endure risk, asset allocation, and diversification are the main aspects of your portfolio.

Investments for different times

Some of the reasons for defining investment goals is to help you know when you will require money to pay for them. The investment method you choose should be different based on the time you invest your money. Goals can be short term, long term, and middle term.

Saving for something big using goals

If you have a dream that you know you can accomplish, if only you had the means, then saving is something that you should consider. To help you realize your dream, below are tips to assist you with the saving part of the equation.

If you only consider debts for true value and investments, you could feel like you don't have the money to accomplish the things you love. However, a smart saving plan may assist you to accomplish all of your dreams. Additionally, you will understand more about your finances.

These tips will help you save between $1,000-$5,000:

1. Create a budget

Your dream may cost more or less, and that is why you need to create a budget in advance. This will help you to outline your plans correctly. Go online and look at existing budgets for projects, trips, and hobbies. Do some research to have a rough idea.

2. Determine your savings rate

You need to know how much you can raise in a day, week, or per pay period. This step has two major sections: monitoring your spending and looking at areas where you can reduce. If you have never monitored your spending before, look for a guide. Monitoring your spending is always a great idea because you will get a rough idea of how much you spend. If you don't have the time, you can approximate by looking at your weekly, monthly, or annual bills.

Once you develop a great idea of your cash flow, find ways to spend less. Saving doesn't mean that you deny yourself everything, so you should not start by being ruthless. But take the time to think of ways in which you can cut down your expenditure without denying yourself the joy of living. Even if it's saving $50, that will add up with time.

> i) A great starting point is your routine bills. Ask yourself what amount of money you want to spend on your internet, car insurance, phone plan, and cable. And how much can you save when you negotiate or go for a less expensive product. The work you put into your savings will pay off after a month.

> ii) Once you review your routine expenses, shift to your discretionary expenses. Small purchases can be quite expensive. If you know where your money is going, then you can decide whether to reduce the cost or go for a cheaper option. If you find it difficult to get a perfect item, ask yourself why you need that product. Maybe the item isn't that important to you, and you could even create a homemade option.

> iii) If cutting down on your spending doesn't seem to work fast, you can think of increasing your income. In this case, you look for ways to earn extra income. You can consider doing some freelance work every week.

> iv)

Determine the period when you will be done with saving

Once you know how much you need, and how fast you can make it, then determining when you will be done shouldn't be hard at all.

Save on autopilot

Until this point, you have accomplished the hard part of building a plan and making tough decisions. What you really need is to move on with your normal life of cutting down on your costs and earning more. The money will slowly increase. It is advised that you spend time every week to evaluate your progress. Saving can include sacrifices if you are going to change your habits of living. Take some time to write down the reasons why you are saving and watch yourself getting closer to your goal.

Be flexible

You may manage to stick to the initial plan. Or you could encounter unexpected challenges. Sometimes, it pays to change your behavior. If the groceries cost more than expected, then it is reasonable to spend less on restaurants.

If you are behind on a goal, or you have to get some money to pay for an emergency, don't be scared; it's simple to adjust. If you think you may need more time, you can update your goal accordingly.

Celebrate

When you achieve your goals, take the time to appreciate your achievement. Savings require persistence and sacrifice. That is why you need to be proud of what you have accomplished.

Chapter 4: Managing Your Personal Finances in a Stress-Free Way

The importance of money management

Do you find yourself with different credit cards, a mortgage, and an auto loan?

There are methods to help you make this manageable. It takes time to discover the ins and outs of it and twist your budget so that it can satisfy your needs:

1. You know where your money is going

Once you budget your money and decide to stick to the budget, you will be able to monitor where your money goes at the end of each month. This is a huge benefit since it will allow you to watch the way you spend money and save more. You can track your spending for several months and then balance the budget to assign a lot of money to savings, or even retirement.

If you handle your money well, you will manage to make early payments, and avoid surpassing the limit on the credit card.

When you stick to your budget, these methods will assist you to save money.

This prevents you from spending much money.

2. A better plan of retirement

When you save now and manage your money in the right way, it will benefit you in the long term. First, it will force you to look into the future and look into your retirement plans.

When you implement your money management skills, you will be building yourself a strong retirement plan. The money that you save and invest will grow as time goes by.

3. Allows you to concentrate on your goals

You will avoid unnecessary expenditure that doesn't support achieving financial goals. If you are dealing with limited resources, budgeting makes it complex to fulfill your ends.

4. You organize your spending and savings

When you divide your income into different types of expenditure and savings, a budget will allow you to remain aware of the type of expenditure that drains the portion of your money. This way, it is simple for you to set adjustments. Good money management acts as a reference for organizing receipts, bills, and financial statements. Once you organize all your financial transactions, you will save effort and time.

5. You can speak to your partner about money

If you do share your income with your spouse, then a budget can be the best tool to show how money is spent. This increases teamwork to work on a common financial target and prevents arguments on the way money is used. Creating a budget together with your spouse will help you to avoid conflict and eliminate personal conflicts on the way money is spent.

6. It determines whether you can take on debt and how much

Taking on debt isn't a bad thing, but it is important, especially if you cannot afford it. A budget will indicate the amount of debt load you can take on without getting stressed.

7. Allows you to generate additional money

When you budget, you get the chance to single out and eliminate unnecessary spendings, such as on penalties, late fees, and interests. These little savings can increase with time.

A budget refers to a plan that takes into account your monthly cash flow and outflow. This is a snapshot of what you own, and what you expect to spend, and which will allow you to realize your financial goals by assisting you in highlighting your saving and spending.

Creating a budget is the most crucial aspect of financial planning. The amount of money you have doesn't indicate how much money you make, but instead, it is how effective your budgeting is. If you want to take care of your finances, then you will have to understand where your money is flowing to. Contrary to popular belief that budgeting is hard, it isn't, and it doesn't eliminate the fun from your life. A budget will save you from an unexpected financial crisis and a life of debt.

Many people have hopes of becoming rich, but they don't have a clue about how to accumulate wealth or where to start. You can begin by learning how to create a budget. A budget is important because it will assist you to start accumulating wealth and accomplishing your goals. Below are some steps to budgeting:

1. Monitor your expenses and income

The first thing to building a budget is to determine the amount of money you have and what you are spending it on. By monitoring your expenses, you will manage to classify how you spend your money. Planning how you spend your money is critical because you can tell how much you want to spend in every category. You can monitor your income and expenses by creating a journal, spreadsheet, or cash book. Every time you make money, you can monitor it as income, and every time you spend money, you can track it as an expense.

If you use a debit card, try to track back three months of your spending to get a comprehensive picture of your expenditure.

2. Evaluate your income

The next stage is to assess your income. You can do this by computing the amount of income you get via gifts, scholarships, etc.

3. Determine your expenses

Once you know your monthly income, next is to determine the total of your expenses. First, you need to define what your fixed, variable expenses are. Fixed expenses, sales, and bills have the same price every month. The fixed expenses comprise of car payments, internet, and rent. Variable expenses refer to costs that change, such as utilities and groceries.

Be sure to include payments of debt in your budget. Find out the amount that you can contribute towards your debts to make sure that you are on the correct path to financial stability. Handling debts and savings go hand in hand.

4. Don't forget about savings

It is quite easy to forget to save money. Keep in mind that you always pay yourself first. Give it a try using 10-20% of your income savings. Since savings increase, you can choose to include money that you didn't spend in the budget to save.

Building a saving strategy

Many people know how to manage the little money they get when the month ends, but they find it hard to save when they have a tight budget. If you look at finance articles online, you will see different types of saving methods—right from freezing all spending to packing your own lunch for a month. But how can you determine which ones work? In this section, you will learn easy money-saving strategies you can implement and how you can make them work for you:

1. Eat out less

It is a fact that eating out is expensive. Even a cup of coffee every day adds up. The cup of coffee may cost you $2, but if you calculate it over a year, that is over $700. In other words, if you continue to eat out every day, you will be spending a lot.

How it works

In a Claris survey, it was found out that 43% of respondents accepted a cutback on eating out, and 33% reported to save money. More than three out of four people who attempted this particular method reported positive results. Though this is not as effective as using a budget, it does save something.

How can you implement it?

If you are eating out every day because you don't know how to cook great food, it is high time that you changed that habit. And don't be worried because learning how to cook is pretty easy. Nowadays, you can turn to YouTube and other online food channels to learn how to prepare different kinds of food. Search for your favorite recipes and begin to follow each step of the preparation.

Remember: cooking food at home doesn't really mean that you need to start everything from scratch. You can choose to purchase chicken broth in a jar. Even if you are going to buy most of these ingredients, a meal prepared at home is going to be cheap.

Even when you have the above ingredients ready, a home prepared meal is cheaper than one from a restaurant.

2. Save loose change

Have a loose change jar. Any time you go shopping and are given coins as change, throw the coins into the jar.

3. Stay out of debt

Being debt free will help you to save cash; if you can pay off all your debt, you will get the chance to organize your debt.

How it works

The stats on eliminating debt can be shocking. For example, the Claris poll showed that only 22% of people attempted this strategy, and 26% reported that it worked for them. In other words, this strategy can help you save money.

Staying out of debt can save you a good sum of cash, but many people find it hard to pay off their debts.

4. Be a minimalist

Adopting a minimalist approach is a type of voluntary simplicity. It requires a person to cut down on costs so that they concentrate on what is important. A minimalist's life generally means owning a smaller house, fewer "toys", and fewer clothes. But it also implies minimal work and more time to do the things that you like.

How does it happen?

This is a great saving strategy that works even for those who don't want to use it. A minimalist approach can be the effect of other methods to save. In most cases, many people scaled their life to stick to their budget. Then, with time, they discovered that their simple lifestyle helped them save more.

How do you do it?

There are various misconceptions about minimalism. A blog about minimalism jokes that minimalists live in small apartments and don't have jobs, cars, TVs, or more than 100 objects.

The purpose of minimalism is to free yourself from issues in life that aren't important. It is not focused on sacrifice; it merely involves eliminating things that you don't want to have in life or creating room for things that you care about. As a result, living with fewer items can make you feel satisfied.

The best thing with living a simple lifestyle is that there is no right or wrong way of doing it. This means that you can become a minimalist by staying in an off-the-grid cabin and make your own food. Or you can stay in an urban loft and walk every day while heading to work. The philosophy of minimalism requires that you concentrate less on the things you have and more on what you do with your life.

If you aren't sure whether you can deal with this kind of life, you can start small and slowly identify a few things in your life that you don't want. For example, if your wardrobe is filled with many things, perhaps throw out or donate some clothes. Or if you spend a lot of time online, plan to reduce your screen time.

Whatever you decide to do, make sure that you don't simplify your life by surrendering on the things you value or treasure; instead, choose things that require the most work for the least reward.

If you are searching for methods to help you save a lot of money, these methods are the best ones to begin with. Since they have worked for other people, there is a big chance that they will work for you too. However, make sure that you don't jump in and try all the methods at once—just select strategies that you believe may work for you.

For example, if you enjoy eating out, as it makes you happy, eliminating this option may not work for you. You will perhaps get disappointed and give up in a few weeks. So, instead of cutting down on eating out, you can decide to look for something different to scale down on.

In general, the purpose is to avoid debt. If your main goal in life is to own a home, don't give up on that and try to avoid a mortgage debt. You can hunt for a house that you will easily manage to pay for, even if it means spending two more years paying for it.

If you aren't sure of the savings style to try, creating a budget is perhaps the best approach. The best thing about budgets is that you don't adjust them to suit your goals; however, you can decide to spend less on your car so that you can get a better house.

Investing your money

Investing your money gives you a chance to grow your money, and even make more than what you have. However, not everyone who decides to invest their money makes profits; some have lost tons of money in the process. There is a different way to invest your money, and this section will introduce you to some of the most common strategies for investment:

Stock investment

If you want to become a stock investor, you need to have a proven strategy for investing in the stock market. You will realize that long-term success begins with learning how to maintain the odds in your favor and control the possible risks.

Understand that for starting investors and seasoned stock market investors, it is impossible to purchase and sell the best stocks at the right time. However, also learn that you don't need to be right to generate money. You simply need to understand the basic rules for how to select the best stocks to watch and the right time to purchase the best stocks at the right time.

Experts in the stock market will tell you that it's hard to time the market, although it's unrealistic to assume that you'll get at the very bottom and out at the very top of a market cycle. There are different methods to identify major changes that occur in the market trends as they arise. When you recognize some of these changes, you can get ready to make substantial profits in a new market.

New investors in the stock market tend to focus on the type of stocks to purchase and ignore the most pertinent issues of when to sell. This is a huge mistake. Without a set of great rules, you might give back all your hard-earned gains.

Typically, there are two major rules that you need to adhere to: the offensive rules of locking your profits, and the defensive rules of cutting down on losses.

Investing online

Online investing can be a quick and convenient method that is more affordable than other methods. But before you can handle your online investment, you need to ask yourself several questions:

What type of investor are you?

Online investing is designed for everyone. By choosing this option, you hold the responsibility to research all investments and make all investment decisions regarding your online account. If you don't feel okay as that kind of investor, you could be comfortable working with a financial advisor. If you like to manage your investment portfolio and feel secure that you have enough knowledge, you may decide to go with online investment.

What type of account do you want to open?

There are various types of online accounts to select from, including joint and individual accounts. The type of account you select will rely on the kind of objectives you have set and how you want to invest.

What company and type of security are you interested in?

For the self-directed investors, it is important to do your homework well because you get some payment for it. There is some level of risk related to all types of investments, so you may want to perform some research to make the right investment decision.

Some tips before investing:

1. Anyone can invest in the stock market, but it's important to save money for retirement and emergencies first.

2. Many people will see significant profits from investing abroad rather than attempting to play the stock market from day to day.

3. If you don't want to trade individual's stocks, begin small, and do your research. Don't just follow advice from famous investors.

Real estate investment

If you want to learn another method to build wealth, then you will have to consider real estate investment. This may seem like an excellent idea, especially if you come from a place where the real estate market is booming. However, you need to be prepared for the commitment.

Real estate demands that you commit your time, and that is why you need to understand it before you start. It is bad to invest in something which you don't have much knowledge about.

Whether real estate investment is a great idea or not, it all depends on you, and your financial abilities. Additionally, your goals will also determine whether you need to invest in real estate. Not every investment is for everyone, but it can be a big tool for growing wealth when done in the right manner.

Types of real estate investment

If you thought that real estate investment is tied only to renting and owning property, then you need to think again. There are basically different methods of investing in real estate, and some of those methods don't require renters.

Ownership of a home

You can purchase a house to invest in. However, there's a slight difference between owning a house and investing in real estate properties. When you invest in a house, you will not make money actively or even increase your monthly cash flow of the property.

The truth is that paying for your house is one of the most important long-term investments you can make.

Invest in Fundrise

Many people want to get into real estate investing, but don't want to handle tenants, repairs, or even manage payments. Fortunately, you can place your money in real estate investment without worrying about doing all the management.

Fundrise is an online investment platform which will give you the chance to invest your cash in real estate investment. It is controlled by Fundrise professionals, while your role is to watch as your money grows.

Why go for Fundrise? It's easy, and they have a track record of excellent returns. Since they can guarantee profits, they are a reputable firm to invest with.

Another reason why most people like to invest with Fundrise is that it's easy to start using it. Also, they will assist you in determining the type of investments that are best for you.

Depending on your response, they will either suggest:

- Long-term growth
- Supplemental income
- Balanced investing

With a minimum of S500, you can invest in Fundrise, or with a minimum of $1,000, you can start to invest in Fundrise income eReit. They have the lowest fees for investment via their site, but the returns are quite reasonable.

Buy rental houses to make income

This is another method you can use to build wealth in the long term. The same reasons why you need to own a home should move you to purchase a property. However, investment in real estate gives you the added advantage of income.

At the least, the rent that you get on investment property has to cover the costs of owning it. When the rent is more than your costs, the property will produce a positive cash flow.

If it does generate a positive cash flow, then the income can come to you as tax-free. The reason is that you can take depreciation expenses on the house. Because it is an investment property, you have permission to "expense" the improvements after some time.

Some things that you should know about rental properties include:

- They require a large down payment, about 20% more of the buying price.

- There are vacancy aspects.

- Repairs and maintenance.

- Earning a mortgage on an investment property rather than the owner-occupied property is hard.

Each of the above factors can be solved, but you must know that owning a property isn't that easy. If you want a lower risk history, rental properties may not be the best investment option for you.

Invest in commercial real estate

This is another variation of rental property which entails investing in retail and office property. It assumes a similar pattern—you buy a property and then rent it out to tenants, who will pay your mortgage and hopefully make some returns.

Commercial real estate investing is generally complicated and expensive compared to investing in rental property in the residential section

But why should you invest in real estate at a commercial level?

The concept of risk versus reward shows that commercial real estate is a lucrative investment because of the huge profits that can be made from it.

On the other hand, commercial real estate usually requires long-term leases. Because the property is going to be rented out as a business, they may require a multi-year lease. This will support the continuity of the business.

Appreciation on a property can also be higher than for residential property. This is prominent when the property generates a large return. And it is likely to be the case for commercial property because the tenant will pay for the maintenance of the building.

Leases can be designed to offer the landlord a given percentage of profits for the business.

The drawback of commercial properties is that they are often subjected to the business cycle. In times of recessions, the business revenue may decrease, and the tenant may have a massive problem in paying for the rent.

Investing in commercial real estate should be for experienced investors who have a huge risk of tolerance.

How to detail your financial goals?

Below are the steps to follow to set up your financial goals:

> 1. Identify what is important to you. Put everything on the table and inspect it.
>
> 2. Filter everything that is within reach, what will require more time, and what should be part of a long-term plan.
>
> 3. Use the SMART goal method.
>
> 4. Develop a realistic budget. Get a clear picture of the flow of your money and then work to focus on that specific goal.
>
> 5. Track your progress.

Examples of financial goals:

1. Create a budget and stick with it.

Some people are shy of the budgeting process. Though you get rich by concentrating on assets and income, experts say that a budget is useful if you want to control how much you spend.

2. Pay off your credit card debt

When setting your financial goals, this should be among your goals. The interest charges on your credit card consume much of your cash flow that could be used somewhere else. Once you clear all your credit card debt, you should be conscious enough not to use the credit card that much.

3. Set up an emergency account

4. Save for your retirement plan

Delayed gratification is a rare feature of many Americans. However, we need to have a retirement plan where we save for the future.

5. Live according to your means

If you do spend more than what you earn, then you will have a lot of debt to pay. If you spend less than your income, you have savings.

6. Nurture skills to increase your income

It doesn't really mean going back to college. It could just mean getting some extra training at your current job. It could also imply looking for a mentor who can deliver tips and feedback. It may also imply going to attend workshops and conferences, or even networking in your job.

7. Have a down payment for your house

For most people, investing in a house is a huge investment. The more the down payment is, the more flexibility and freedom will be given for the entire period of the loan.

8. Increase your credit score

For you to get that house or any other purchase that needs a loan, you have to qualify for a much lower interest rate. In other words, a high credit score saves you a lot of money to be eligible for lower interest rates.

The main point is that everyone can do more than what they think they can, and we need to plan for our financial future.

Accomplishing your financial goals

The right way to achieve your goals is to generate a plan that will prioritize your goals.

When you review your goals, you will realize that some are narrow while others are broad. You can classify your goals into:

1. Short-term financial goals, which require less than a year to accomplish. An example is purchasing a new refrigerator.

2. Mid-term goals can be realized instantly but should not take many years to achieve. Examples include completing a degree and buying a car.

3. Long-term goals may take many years to achieve. Examples include buying a house and saving for a child's college education.

The process of setting goals requires making a decision of the type of goals you want to achieve and approximating the size of money needed and other needed resources.

Create a goal chart

Creating a financial goal chart is the best way to begin your process of investment. Below are five steps that can be useful to help you build your goal chart:

1. Note down your financial goal. It has to be measurable, specific, realistic, and contain a timeline.

2. Determine whether you have set a short-term, mid-term, or long-term goal. This can change depending on your condition.

3. Determine the amount of money that you need to achieve your goal.

4. Brainstorm methods that you can use to attain your goal while cutting down on your expenses.

5. Choose the best ways to fulfill your goals and note them down.

Conclusion

Your credit score will affect your potential purchasing of significant items, such as a car or house. As a result, it is important to have a healthy credit score that will deliver to you the freedom to enjoy life. If you have a bad credit score, and you want to build it back to a good score, first, you have to know what you are working with. Look for a copy of your credit report via different free sources. Once you have the copy, look for errors and open account balances.

When you have a good credit score, you tend to have peace of mind and can start saving for the future. Saving for your future is critical, and that is why you need to begin "thinking lean", which will show you opportunities to become creative and reduce your expenditure.

Keep in mind that by saving today, you will be preparing for a great future when you grow old. Now that you have come to the end of the book don't stop now—start putting into practice everything that you have learned. Creating a budget, setting your financial goals, and eliminating things that eat out your expenditure is the sure way to realize the objectives of this book.